instant
karma

8,879 WAYS TO GIVE YOURSELF AND OTHE
GOOD FORTUNE RIGHT NOW

BARBARA ANN KIPFER

Workman Publishing ▮ New York

Library of Congress Cataloging-in-Publication Data
Kipfer, Barbara Ann.
Instant Karma / Barbara Ann Kipfer.
p. cm.
ISBN: 0-7611-2804-2 (alk. paper)
1. Conduct of life. I. Title

BF637.C5K56 2003
291.4'4—dc21   2003041067

Workman books are available at special discounts when purchased in bulk for premiums and sales promotions as well as for fund-raising or educational use. Special editions or book excerpts can also be created to specification. For details, contact the Special Sales Director at the address below.

Workman Publishing Company, Inc.
708 Broadway
New York, NY 10003-9555
www.workman.com

Printed in United States of America

First printing April 2003

10 9 8 7 6 5 4

To Paul, who provides the balancing force
in my life, and my two big boys, Kyle and Keir,
who enliven it. We climb mountains and reach
for the stars, strengthening the love we share.
Thank you for everything.

Special thanks to senior editor Jennifer Griffin,
assistant editor Cindy Schoen, designer Elaine Tom,
production editor Doug Wolff, and to my publisher,
Peter Workman. It is wonderful to have the
opportunity to work with you.

INTRODUCTION

Instant Karma is a collection of thousands of ways to create good karma for yourself and others. The advice here is based on the principles of Buddhism, Taoism, and other spiritual traditions, and it emphasizes the importance of physical health, spiritual growth, harmony, and peace. *Instant Karma* is full of simple, immediate suggestions to enliven and enlighten your life. I try to incorporate these ideas into my everyday life, and I hope you'll find ideas here that you'll want to incorporate into yours.

The book encompasses four fundamental principles of spirituality: karma, dharma, yoga, and tao. Karma is cause and effect: what you do today, good or bad, comes back to you tomorrow. Dharma means cosmic law—we practice dharma to be in tune with nature and the world. Yoga is more than stretching the body—it is enlightenment through movement. Tao is the practice of acting in harmony with the fundamental essence of everything you encounter. All of these principles and the many more traditions you find here are meant to open your heart and rekindle your spirit, celebrate the present, and help you gain mental and physical strength.

You can read *Instant Karma* from start to finish, or you can open it to any page for a pick-me-up. The nature of the book is meant to allow you to discover something new every time you read it. Many of the entries will speak to you today; others will ring true years from now; some may never fit your life. That's okay. Take what you want and leave the rest.

There are an infinite number of ways to make improvements in your life and the lives of others. This is just a beginning. What can you do to improve your and others' karma?

- wait for a door to be unlocked instead of trying to break it down
- test your intelligence by challenging it
- put a rug down for bare feet
- stop work at your computer and place your hands in *namaste,* the centered position of respect and thanks
- give the best information
- initiate a program of social reform
- learn from the natural, relaxed way in which young children move
- enjoy your eccentricities and those of other people
- on a gloomy day, put sunny yellow napkins on the table
- believe that the best is yet to be
- put something extra in someone's piggy bank
- take up an expressive form of dance
- surrender/trust
- volunteer at your child's school

 instant karma

- be self-reliant
- learn to see desires and make choices rather than act on all of them
- live the examined life
- know the purpose for which you are reading
- give away a tenth of your income to charities and good causes
- if you wish to secure peace for yourself, start by championing it for others
- do not take life's experiences too seriously
- make creativity a way of life
- trust and embrace the organic pattern of your life
- name a star for a friend's birthday gift
- introduce dietary changes gradually
- try not to do everything at once
- enter a contest—you may win!
- give the pet a sponge bath
- build a model car with a child

- approach the day's tasks with reverence
- support your alma mater
- read a mammoth unabridged dictionary
- build a tree house for a child
- celebrate good food from the earth
- repeat the sacred words of great teachers
- love — and let the rest go
- challenge yourself to "make do"
- stop holding your breath and begin breathing from your diaphragm
- get new underwear and socks on a regular basis
- balance strenuous mental activity with physical work or exercise
- use meetings sparingly and always stick to an agenda
- experience the fact that you are alive, a presence in the here and now
- make your kitchen the most comfortable room in the house

- show personal integrity
- don't risk what you don't want to lose
- call or write your cousins
- improvise when necessary
- only love dispels hate
- spread a little joy
- enjoy a wide variety of foods
- thank the person at theaters who tears tickets
- imagine living your life without being afraid to take a risk
- invite guests to your place of worship
- life is positive; only your thinking is negative
- Boldness has genius, power, and magic in it (Johann Wolfgang von Goethe)
- light a candle for someone you're concerned about
- take the focus off yourself
- make life move at a more leisurely pace
- put yourself in someone else's shoes

- go to the midnight church service on Christmas Eve
- make a habit of reading something inspiring and cheerful just before going to sleep
- the more attention you bring to eating, the more interesting it becomes
- give your best self to the world
- give someone a back rub
- do not expect praise or reward
- make two casseroles and bring one to a friend
- welcome immigrants who work hard
- eat only until you are no longer hungry
- work to music
- help someone assemble the ingredients for cooking
- make bird feeders to encourage avian visitors
- do less; be more
- live according to your beliefs
- rent a bike on your vacation
- send a hand-delivered telegram of love

- help preserve one-room schoolhouses
- donate your old sets of children's books to a library
- a vegetarian diet is in harmony with *ahimsa,*
  or nonviolence
- learn to be your own counselor
- sometimes you have to stay in the kitchen even if you
  don't like the heat—think of it as a karmic test
- create a sense of joy everywhere you go
- take a baby terrarium to a shut-in
- have the generosity to allow others what they deserve
- know emergency numbers
- take your morning coffee break with a compassionate
  coworker
- keep your food simple
- create your ultimate to-do list, one that helps you chart
  your path
- listen to the whole answer
- clean your house with all-natural ingredients

- regardless of the situation, react with class
- tame your appetite
- equip a guest room with toiletries and a robe
- less is usually more
- let things unfold in their own time
- why judge?
- remember that how you say something is as important as what you say
- good scientists free themselves of concepts and keep their minds open to what is
- recognize ordinary, everyday activities as opportunities to awaken
- demonstrate your dedication to your partner in public
- improve your posture
- take care of your mind and body
- fill out the "How was the service?" card
- refuse to tell a lie, even a small one
- organize a group to practice sitting meditation

- cheer up a dreary desk with flowers
- luck lies all around: all you need to do is pick up the blessings on your path
- choose to direct the course and quality of your life
- take the time to help a stranger who needs directions
- whatever you cultivate during good times becomes your strength during bad times
- be comfortable with ambiguity
- provide a sustaining hot breakfast on a cold winter morning
- teach your kids to eat healthfully
- A crust eaten in peace is better than a banquet partaken in anxiety (Aesop)
- respect tradition
- reflect on the kindness of everyone you meet
- breathe deeply to calm the emotions and relax the nerves
- care about the happiness of others

- support soapbox derby racing
- go for a morning run with good friends
- be gentle and patient with an angry person
- make time for meditation
- spot for someone who is bench-pressing
- smile at the person in the car next to you
- when wishes are few, the heart is happy
- when you get home, kick off your shoes
- buy a red carnation and wear it to work
- chew consciously
- make time for yourself
- give as much as you have received
- master a skill
- know when to quit
- treat animals well
- donate crossword-puzzle books to hospitals
- make a doggie birthday cake with ground lamb and creamy oatmeal

- trust those on whom you depend, and care for those who depend on you
- offer to run an errand for your spouse
- learn the art of compromise
- explore the richness of your imperfections
- change your routines
- start your family's day by making fresh orange juice
- keep your dealings aboveboard
- keep your relationships in good shape
- make honesty your only policy
- silence is sometimes the best answer
- dream nice dreams
- make sure your words reflect your compassion
- nurture your kids
- take a garbage bag on your walk and clean up after others
- buy two copies of a book so you can read it with your sweetheart

- live your life with integrity, compassion, and a healthy sense of humor
- turn feelings of kindness into action
- keep your eyes on the goal
- eat your favorite comfort food for dinner
- begin to experience the difference between love and attachment, between loss and grief
- get someone a welcome-back present
- find your work meaningful
- don't worry about an unpleasant task, just do it right now
- shift the tone of a gripe session with jokes and humor
- give away knowledge to acquire knowledge
- no matter how much goodness you do, do more
- ask for help when you need it
- when you accept yourself just as you are, then you can change
- try a TV fast

- shop at the local health food store
- go slow and soft
- serve meals to the homeless on a holiday
- Zen will bring perspective to your life by illuminating your ability to pay attention to everything with equal fervor
- when you come to a dead end, turn up another street
- make things happen quietly
- build a house out of recycled materials
- look at things from someone else's perspective
- play relaxing music during dinner
- make busy-day meals pleasant
- share your love of books
- see everything in your life as a gift
- increase your vocabulary to strengthen your mental circuitry
- give your spouse all you can
- associate with winners

- learn to do things for yourself
- play with your kids on Saturday
- put your jacket around someone on a chilly evening
- keep a stash of toys for young visitors
- don't make your appearance more important than your disposition
- supply calculators or dictionaries to needy schoolchildren
- show a child how to use a fire extinguisher
- make sure all your friends get home safely from holiday parties
- make lots of good changes
- make kindness your true religion
- draw with children
- allow your day to unfold
- knowledge of your chakras will help you pinpoint the problem areas of your life and provide a basis for personal growth

 instant karma

- leave a small surprise gift in the refrigerator
- bring a coloring book and crayons for a young child at a restaurant
- pray for the welfare of a friend or family member
- believe inner peace is possible
- look forward to the prospect of learning
- do good
- write down three things that were great about today
- think of others
- teach a child to read
- resolve to take only what your body needs
- make every room of your home comfortable
- upon retiring, sleep as if you had entered your last sleep
- think multipurpose, not single-purpose
- bear all cheerfully
- begin each meal by giving thanks, even silently
- surprise someone with their favorite sandwich

- find the silver lining in the cloud
- pay your bills on time
- research your options
- respond to a hug
- make a difference
- use sunscreen
- acknowledge the reality of the times
- practice the "letting-go mind"
- start out someone's day with a joke or funny story
- buy a fan a ticket to the Indianapolis 500
- practice a steady obedience to what you know to be right
- discover your own quiet joy
- know that you're doing the best you can — for now
- invite a loved one to snuggle
- Life does not need to be changed; only our intents and actions do (Swami Rama)
- Zen asks that you empty your mind

- buy used books whenever possible
- grow old gracefully
- remember that understanding karma is the key to understanding happiness
- go out on a limb to get the fruit on the tree
- nurture these qualities: precision, gentleness, and the ability to let go
- only watch television programs you are really interested in
- give a book that makes someone smile or laugh
- exude peace when those around you are anxious
- grow herbs in a window garden
- before you say something, ask yourself whether your words will build or harm the relationship?
- get automobile brochures for someone considering a new car purchase
- go to the library and become a student
- simplify

- listen to Beethoven's Ninth
- help ban nuclear anything
- give someone a picnic for their airplane trip
- help a girl perfect her cartwheel
- each week, watch one fewer television show
- master the moment
- win public office and make good on your promises
- bring someone a bunch of violets
- dance in the summer rain
- buy coffee and breakfast for the person behind you at the coffee shop
- teach children by (good) example
- how can you quarrel — knowing that life is as fleeting as a flash of lightning?
- deliver compassion
- drop a dollar where someone will find it
- bring plants and flowers, with their healing yang energy, into a convalescing person's bedroom

- buy from charity bake sales
- experience life and death in each moment
- get to know your kids
- complete a project
- set up pictures of your family in your hotel room
- create circumstances that make you smile
- finish each mouthful of food before reaching for another
- arise one hour earlier in the morning and practice yoga or martial arts
- clean the garage even if it's not your chore
- be humble about your good fortune
- practice your faith
- value yourself
- laugh uproariously with children
- make a dedication on a local radio station to all those who smiled at strangers that day
- acknowledge your own positive features and qualities

- **dig up a couch potato**
- choose a salad over a steak
- see both sides
- plant a kiss on someone's palm and roll the fingers to "hold" it for later use
- honey-coat your words
- offer compassion and support to a suffering friend
- don't try to buy happiness
- accept yourself as you are, body and soul
- pull more than your weight
- help someone work on a project
- take from your employer only what is given
- leave the mind in its natural undisturbed state
- use your yoga practice to feel your emotions on a physical level — then you can move past them
- plant evergreens
- practice listening — we don't learn anything new when we are speaking

- visit the children's ward at a hospital
- forgive people their imperfections at every opportunity
- give your partner assurance of your commitment
- all your actions and comments come back to you
- think like a kid
- make everyday meals a celebration of abundance
- appreciate the fragrance of a summer rose, the last glow of the fireplace
- mutually exchange knowledge, kindness, service, celebration
- say no consciously
- just let yourself "be" for five minutes — or as long as you can
- try not to take your work concerns home with you
- seek the essence of beauty every day
- use yoga to help you release your inner delight
- wake early to give yourself a head start on the day

- decorate for the holidays with items that make you smile
- share what you have learned
- retrain your mind to heighten its awareness of each of the senses
- listen critically and thoughtfully
- turn in cans and bottles for the deposit money
- remove a splinter for someone
- go apple-picking
- don't be immersed in the future
- develop extraordinary powers of observation
- look for possibilities, not limits
- become the moment and put all else out of your mind
- be in charge of your feelings
- give milestone gifts — like fifty golf balls for turning fifty
- be a mentor to a young person who admires you
- eat foods that will keep you healthy

- provide a frog or turtle with safe crossing to the other side of the street
- let go of the past
- soften your most stubborn opinions
- skip one restaurant meal a week and give the money you would have spent to charity
- don't try to blame, reason, or argue
- exercise awareness over your reactions to people you have an instinctive aversion to
- change self-defeating behavior
- be a connoisseur of language
- bring breakfast fixings over to a friend's house and cook something together
- be honest about your limitations
- help a community rebuild after a flood
- observe God's precepts
- enhance even the most mundane aspects of life with beauty

- offer someone warm milk before bedtime
- **help keep grandparents young**
- stay aware of the fact that everything is in ceaseless change
- discover your work, and then give yourself to it with all your heart
- learn to connect with others
- start exercising today
- ask questions that others will enjoy answering
- learn more about deep breathing
- listen carefully to your customers or clients
- the more you do for others, the happier you will be
- make sure you have everything you need before you start a project
- direct your mind to the present moment whenever you feel sluggish
- bury a time capsule that will delight its discoverer
- put forth your best effort

- believe the best of everybody
- put things away
- send your mom a corsage, your dad a boutonniere
- take a family hike
- do something that will put a smile on your face
- decide not to worry about it
- hunt for new ways to see and create beauty
- have a friend's favorite book bound in leather
- never deprive someone of hope
- sleep avidly and dream vividly
- ask to be removed from mailing lists
- indulge in joy
- value what you do and do what you value
- be modest
- deepen your relationship with nature and find greater contentment
- do what you loved to do as a child
- do Pilates rollups to keep your spine flexible

- build a comfortable cushion of savings
- begin each day saying, "I am awake and grateful to be alive"
- share things: toys, fun, giggles, secrets
- turn kids on to the sciences
- talk about what is bothering you instead of getting angry when others cannot read your mind
- rent an RV and go on a road trip
- Look wise, say nothing, and grunt; speech was given to conceal thought (Sir William Osler)
- take in a stray puppy
- use what you have
- applaud the piano player in a restaurant
- see with your inner eye, hear with your inner ear
- do *metta*: May [name] be filled with loving kindness. May [name] be well. May [name] be peaceful and at ease. May [name] be happy.
- do less running around

- observe the senses to see what attracts and repels you
- nothing worthwhile is achieved overnight
- buy comfortable furniture
- use the "sweeping" technique of observing sensations throughout the body
- become a handyperson
- be up and about early in the day
- be inconspicuous
- bake a pie for your mother-in-law
- say grace before each meal
- if you try, you might surprise yourself
- refuse to listen to others gripe and complain
- repeat activities that increase your self-esteem
- give your partner love and fidelity, but also authority
- be quiet for a moment, until the right words arise by themselves
- give books to the poor
- make your home a sanctuary

- give the gift of undivided attention
- cut your neighbors' grass while they're away
- buy school supplies for a needy child
- give Dad a bucket of new golf balls
- sponsor the street block party
- shake up your routine
- eat fruit instead of bacon and eggs for breakfast
- lighten up — you will live longer
- consider yourself fortunate
- designate a day each week to leave your car at home
- to quiet a worrying mind, imagine a hive surrounded by honeybees, each bee representing a niggling problem; visualize the bees disappearing one at a time into the hive and notice how your mind quiets
- give small treasures found in nature
- surprise someone with a special event
- use every moment skillfully
- ask, how can I help?

- learn to flow
- be firm but courteous to telemarketers
- turn off your gray matter when exercising
- softly prop someone up in bed
- do more with less
- everything is possible!
- work according to seasonal circumstances
- meditate at the health club
- go the extra mile for your clients
- detachment is sometimes the greatest act of love
- explore anything that interests you
- write an unexpected letter
- meet the circumstances around you
- realize there is nothing lacking, and the whole world belongs to you
- pay attention
- bring a sense of adventure to a children's birthday party

- become more peaceful with where you are in life
- learn something from every experience
- have control over your thoughts to have control over your speech
- bring out the best in everyone
- act consciously and intentionally
- develop your own philosophy
- do the least harm possible
- share a chair
- leave space in your stomach when eating
- there is always time to do what is important
- only here and now can you truly love — the past is a memory, the future is a fantasy
- care enough about yourself to set limits
- encourage people to share their excitement about life
- What do we live for, if it is not to make life less difficult for each other? (George Eliot)
- share a TV show with someone

- love yourself
- be courteous
- acknowledge your successes
- serve as an example
- show praise and appreciation
- teach children that people matter more than things
- invite someone to breakfast
- try to keep your meals on a regular schedule
- live quietly
- make time for uninterrupted leisure
- take courses at your local college or university
- once you set a goal, stick to the goal, not necessarily to the details of the plan
- There's only one corner of the universe you can be certain of improving and that's your own self. So you have to begin there, not outside, not on other people. (Aldous Huxley)
- be a peaceful person to have a peaceful home

- take time to discuss the events of the day with your mate
- adopt the pace of nature
- allow others more space, freedom, and time
- read about fashion in magazines — then wear whatever you want
- remember that love is not leisure, it is work
- take the training wheels off and ride!
- respect other people's solitude
- listen to your mind; learn to be aware of your actions
- practice makes patterns and etches habits into our cells
- show gratitude to yourself
- take care of each moment
- unwind for a few days — or a summer, or your favorite season!
- find the funny side of a situation
- live a spiritual life, and you will have less fear of death

- consider first the end
- spend more time reading
- let events take their course
- before you get up, reflect on what it means to wake up and meet the day
- bear an injustice without retaliating
- appreciate brilliance
- have a variety of places to walk
- walk around earthworms on the street after a warm spring rain
- develop playful reactions to problems
- attend a church supper
- have more fun than anyone else
- don't seek love; seek all the barriers within yourself that you have built against it
- when you ask people how they are, really listen to the response
- live your own life

- try to be an informed consumer
- be long on confidence
- put a condiment smile on a kid's sandwich or burger
- unwind with the fragrance of a vanilla-scented candle
- you are exactly where you're meant to be
- ignore setbacks and refuse to give up
- let Furies become Muses
- turn your garden into a showplace
- eliminate the meaningless chatter from your communication
- polish a pregnant woman's toenails
- groom yourself religiously
- believe it and then you will see it
- forgive yourself and others
- cherish your children for what they are
- even if you cannot sleep — rest
- try a centering prayer: the silent repetition of a word or phrase, used as a focus point

- above all else, choose good health
- buck the status quo
- do less thinking and pay more attention to your heart
- read a guide on money management
- first think, then speak
- admire gardens
- don't get upset by confusion
- invite the neighbors for a cookout
- pay attention to traditional values
- We never do anything well till we cease to think about the manner of doing it (William Hazlitt)
- look out into the far horizon and up to the sky at least once a day
- make a tape of favorite songs for your partner
- try it someone else's way
- instead of being upset when something is broken or destroyed, try to feel grateful for the time you had it
- eradicate meanness

- learn something about a family member's special interest
- if you don't need it, don't buy it
- campaign for universal health care
- thank the trash collector
- avoid exaggeration
- eat more fiber
- talk pleasantly with receptionists
- if you are not able to speak calmly, don't speak
- when you have doubts about what to do, just imagine that today is your last day, and then you will see clearly what your conscience tells you
- see life's big picture
- notice changes
- be comfortable with contradictory ideas in your mind
- turn repetitive actions into refreshing experiences
- for one week, try to improve one area of your life
- be someone's cheerleader

 instant karma

- once you have unstuffed a space, do not bring more stuff into it
- try indoor rock-climbing
- join hands at midnight on New Year's Eve and say a special prayer for the coming year
- practice waiting patiently
- remain open to experience and change
- expand the boundaries of your knowledge
- you already have what you are looking for
- play classical music for children as they go to sleep
- help paint a room
- mindfulness takes away worries and fears about past and future and keeps us anchored in the present
- make a list of all your important documents and where they are for your loved ones
- open air and sun are good for your health (but don't forget the sunblock!)
- pick up after others rather than nag

- be quiet in a library
- rather than paddling up the river, flow with it
- rake your neighbor's yard
- offer suggestions for town improvements
- give your very best
- think about today — don't think about doing something or anything forever
- improve your family environment
- conscious walking lets you practice staying on track
- relieve anger, anxiety, and depression by altering harmful habits of thought
- revive a lost art form
- support a petting zoo for children
- practice feng shui
- share goodies with other campers or picnickers
- learn to tell a joke
- the way we choose to see the world creates the world we see

- chew your food well to prevent bad breath
- contribute something unique to the world
- focus on what's important
- seize the happy moments
- do an eye-palming exercise and notice brighter colors and sharper, more defined objects
- lose some of your armor — invite and allow others to share your experience
- go home for the holidays
- ask people not to give you a gift but rather to give to someone who needs it
- use yoga to soothe the nerves and calm the body
- take some lemon and honey in the morning
- drive around to look at Christmas lights and decorations
- read scriptures and holy books
- take the initiative — don't wait for the other person to apologize

- don't waste time responding to critics
- laugh at everyone's jokes
- realize all things change; don't try to hold on
- learn Morse code
- offer to take an elderly neighbor to the supermarket when you shop
- band together as neighbors to help a neighbor in need
- master a new gadget
- move anything that prevents doors from opening fully
- be quick to do good deeds
- make a PBJ from whole-grain bread, freshly ground natural peanut butter, and fruit-sweetened jam
- try to be the voice of reason and reconciliation
- chat with a dear friend
- be aware of the sensation of the breath
- introduce daily self-massage into your routine
- find the positive side of a situation

- use your walks as a vigorous focused meditation to close the distance we often imagine between body and mind
- write letters to representatives in Washington, D.C.
- be one with the dharma
- assume good intent
- have fun along the way
- reward a great baby-sitter
- improve your marriage for your children's sake
- decide on a fun sideline project
- acknowledge that everything in your life matters
- welcome well-behaved children
- don't require verbal thanks
- sponsor a child
- celebrate the imperfections of your relationships
- take time to pray
- be endlessly curious about the universe
- use your bonus airline miles to send someone on a trip

- go do something interesting
- invent your own recipe for living
- practice consciously doing one thing at a time
- relax
- don't put on an act
- don't jump to conclusions
- when you are truthful, you will be trusted
- respect those who have a different focus
- change your worst personality trait
- think ahead so the last of life is the dessert
- to say you love someone is not enough
- take lots of notes in the classroom
- savor the moment
- accumulate wisdom with age
- lend a hand to a sibling
- drink lots of water
- as you eat, bring wholehearted attentiveness to taste, smell, and sensation

- learn the skills of intimacy
- find a meaningful career
- practice portion control when eating
- learn what the animal world has to teach
- if a generous thought occurs to you, act on it
- negotiate solutions to crises
- every day, look for some small way to improve your marriage
- give good foot rubs
- find a job compatible with your basic values
- develop the ability to wait and to listen
- be patient
- take a favorite friend to lunch
- sit with an important question as a contemplation exercise
- change the way you have always done something
- ask yourself, is my life in balance?
- see beauty in the simple

- take time to reach out to others
- celebrate life's little accomplishments
- clean your cupboards of all the pots, pans, utensils, dishes, and appliances you don't use
- know when to bite your tongue
- freedom is found in a life where there is little choice
- make a picnic special, packing the favorite foods of your companions
- choose the best response
- base your choices on what you know today
- learn how to use aromas to influence your mood
- listen to your body before every meal and determine what you actually want to eat
- love the rainy days, too
- think of overhauling your diet as an adventure
- believe in the supreme worth of the individual
- donate to AIDS research
- win the affection of children

- know when to rest
- pay full attention to what you are doing
- let go completely to find complete peace
- take yourself to lunch
- tell a teenager something you wish you had known at his or her age
- participate in a walkathon as a family
- get a library card for a young friend
- dedicate your day to an idea — and every hour try to bring yourself back to that idea
- each time you acknowledge a state of mind without judgment, it weakens the state of mind and strengthens the ability to let go
- watch home movies or slides together
- stay the race until the end
- visit hospitals with smiles and friendly conversation for patients
- let a kid read late into the night

- know the names of your senators and representatives
- be common in nothing
- go into stillness and wait
- keep your secrets
- reduce your meat consumption
- consider life and death equal
- remind yourself of core values by creating personal rituals
- do simple things to make your home and your work space more beautiful
- behave during the day in such a way that you can sleep at night in peace
- maintain your Buddha mind as you work
- stroke a dog's ears
- relish small pleasures
- send all of your cousins a greeting card
- don't react when you are in a disagreeable mood
- have "real" conversations with family and friends

- expect to hear some good news every day
- put framed family pictures in all rooms of the house
- mental noting (labeling your thoughts) helps you not to take the contents of your thoughts too seriously
- dedicate your life to spiritual perfection
- let frustrations become occasions to practice patience
- befriend people from other countries
- write a letter to someone you care about who is no longer in your life
- There is no beginning too small (Henry David Thoreau)
- imagine never having to regret anything you say!
- go for whole grain
- listen to your body and work toward instinctively consuming a healthful diet
- harmonize your actions with the way life really is
- turn the constraints of your situation to your advantage

- pay attention!
- learn how other people see things
- be kind to yourself and others
- mindfulness makes every moment count
- allow others a place in your space
- exercise for as much time each day as you spend eating
- collect uncirculated pennies for a child
- act in a wholesome way
- don't let others interfere with your resolve to live a full, productive day
- when your mind wanders from what you are doing, bring it back
- recognize illusions as illusions and fantasies as fantasies
- embrace each change of the seasons
- uniting a spiritual practice with a necessity (like eating) catalyzes the process of becoming aware of things, or intentionality

- make the best of the way things turn out
- be a reading parent who has reading children
- remain patient in spite of provocation
- do a genealogy chart for a sibling
- let go of unrealistic expectations
- expect the best from others
- buy the Little Leaguers hot dogs after the game
- support the animal rights movement
- write a letter to the editor
- let friends surprise you
- wait an hour or two after eating to lift weights
- request the pleasure of a dance
- soothe your inner crank
- praise other people's children
- curiosity inspires creativity
- if you accept and learn not to criticize yourself, you will find true health — physical, mental, and spiritual
- allow the flavor of goodness to permeate your life

- do not give in to your emotions
- practice silence of the heart by loving, and by avoiding selfishness, hatred, jealousy, and greed
- wink at your stress; we all know you aren't so important
- let go of what is no longer helpful
- bring some poetry with you wherever you go
- celebrate near-perfect weather
- get up early one day a week and take yourself to breakfast
- live your faith
- when under stress, keep your workout light
- lie flat on your back with legs relaxed open, your arms by the sides of your body, palms open and up (Corpse Pose)
- control your emotions
- fit in small amounts of exercise throughout the day
- empty your mind during a walk

- resolve to maintain a balance in everyday life
- even after you think your exhalation is done, push out a bit more
- don't eat out of sadness or anger
- be your partner's best friend and biggest fan
- set the atmosphere of your home by listening to uplifting, positive, or relaxing music
- do your job well
- drink vegetable juice
- adopt a pet from the Humane Society
- be a source of love
- give youth a sense of security, importance, and responsibility
- let your mind be restless
- forgive your past mistakes and move on
- let people enjoy life in their own ways
- put more value on people than on stuff or ideas
- build a cozy fire in the wintertime

- a vegetarian diet uses approximately fifteen times less water than a meat-based diet
- guess positively when you are not sure
- start choosing water instead of other beverages until it becomes a habit
- bring closure to troubles
- give yourself a pat on the back
- take dirty or wet shoes off outside before coming into the house
- one good thing leads to another
- observe anti-litter laws
- try harder
- practice some belief, philosophy, or religion each day
- take a little time to think about what you are doing and why you are doing it
- use a kitchen scale to learn the size of reasonable portions
- attend an Earth Day celebration

- begin to see aging as a natural process
- be peaceful
- buy and cook fresh food whenever you can
- be moderate in your views
- eating mindfully is an important aspect of meditation
- frame a wedding invitation as a present to the couple
- see the world as a friendly place
- love thy neighbor as thyself
- keep your eyes open for all things good
- have the flexibility to make midcourse corrections
- for one day, pay attention to how you reach for, use, and discard things
- say hello to people in an elevator
- fill notebooks with affirmations and positive quotes
- learn CPR
- enjoy free community resources — libraries, talks, etc.
- wear down what's on the surface of ordinary life to expose what you really feel

- do it now!
- steady your karma through meditation
- use mind-mapping (putting thoughts on a paper map) to think, work, and problem-solve in less time
- place an energetic fountain near your front door to encourage good to enter
- before you eat, ask yourself if you are really hungry
- be balanced in everything you do
- resist the urge to multitask
- practice listening to others
- protect family heirlooms
- arrange a bulldozer ride for a child
- donate a tree to a local park
- write or draw your anger away
- in governing, don't try to control
- throw away your junk
- experience your angry feelings, but don't react to them right away

- follow directions
- try to do creative work before your habitual chores
- toss out last year's accumulated guilt
- analyze your life closely
- save money
- if you want to know what your future life will look like, look at your life right now
- treat everyone with civility and respect
- exhibit community leadership
- carefully examine what you are dishing out
- present an inexpensive but thoughtful gift in an elaborate package
- one step starts each journey
- remember the joy of cooking
- cherish your dreams
- start a gratitude list
- don't look for recognition
- recognize and value your mistakes

- fight inertia
- keep medicine out of the reach of children
- have faith in your own ideas
- plant the seeds of the Buddha's Right View —
  the absence of all views — in children
- create your own lexicon
- be comfortable with your body — you will exude
  confidence and beauty
- delight in each moment of awakening
- ask yourself, what's really important?
- go antiques-hunting with your mother-in-law
- provide free books to schools
- reinstate the ritual of afternoon tea
- the more you concentrate, the fewer the causes
  of agitation and the more peaceful your mind
- do a family or group art project
- try following your breath while listening to music
- build a legacy that is respected

55 instant karma

- control the thoughts and images that flash through your mind
- lend a hand
- if you are feeling low, try looking up
- make up the bed with fragrant rose petals tucked between the sheets
- hold a garage sale to rid your home of clutter
- talk about ideals, not people or things
- face life
- be kind to animals
- be devoted to something outside yourself
- ask, do I want to act on this thought, or just watch it pass through?
- let your upset mind settle
- buy yourself a bouquet of flowers
- monitor your feelings
- show an interest in your child's friends
- aim for an A on every test

- do not despise what you cannot have
- find religion
- map out a strategy for realizing your ideal hobby
- regard your life as an extended working vacation
- always try to see yourself through God's eyes
- call your children from work just to say hi
- make your house look welcoming on the outside
- don't laugh when someone makes a mistake
- be punctual
- burn candles
- eat natural foods more often
- take nothing for granted
- learn to judge the quality of a food by its aroma
- question "conventional wisdom"
- practice rugged individualism
- use your ears to explore the world
- praise children often
- preserve old family movies, slides, and photos

- rely on yourself to honestly monitor the quality and progress of your practice
- loosen your tendency to control
- create a silly diversion in your day
- honor a "Do Not Disturb" sign
- kiss your mate wildly
- meditate with perseverance
- let your workings remain a mystery; just show people the results
- buy recycled paper
- plant a garden you can eat from
- embrace change
- don't cry over spilt milk
- just breathe
- try a new cuisine
- savor whatever comes your way
- buy a poppy from a veteran
- be wary of trendy magazines that focus on simplicity

- give up your attachments to the rules, plans, and other details of life
- you have the option to act on your thoughts — or not
- outwardly go along with the flow; inwardly keep your true nature
- teach within the home
- list ten things you can do to add beauty to your life that cost little or no money
- trust your own way of doing things
- open your eyes to the greatness of your world
- do not react or speak — be like a tree
- give up a half hour of TV every day
- do not be led by hearsay
- let everything feed your spirit
- clear your mind
- let kids lick the batter bowl
- give the gift of enthusiasm
- use positive self-talk from morning until bedtime

- treat yourself with generosity
- remind yourself that there is more to life than simple achievement
- become more centered, balanced, straightforward, and calm
- believe in yourself and your dreams
- encounter all creations with respect and dignity
- have a tender heart in any situation
- do the right thing even when no one is looking
- don't plan for any particular result
- be a team player
- loving-kindness is more powerful and effective than anger
- drive to a park, listen to the birds, smell the grass
- life is too important to take too seriously
- expect to love and cherish your spouse for as long as you both shall live
- keep a well-stocked home tool kit

- heal your sorrows and wounds with compassion
- dig out a piece of lawn and put in a garden
- admit to things that you do not know
- keep a record of good things that happen
- spend one day in silence
- keep the generations connected
- garden with a child
- practice conscious restraint
- give a graduate a well-deserved vacation
- praise a child's achievements
- practice mindfulness for at least five minutes every morning
- focus on the moment rather than on dreams or regrets
- read yoga tips to improve your practice
- have the fearless attitude of a hero and the loving heart of a child
- give yourself to the journey

- polish someone's shoes as a surprise gesture of love
- make the best of bad situations
- the more you give love, the more love you have to give
- expend the bulk of your energy planting good roots today
- resolve each day to change a behavior
- remember the blessings in your life
- spend some quiet time outside in the fresh air
- determine to speak truthfully, with words that inspire self-confidence, joy, and hope
- remain in the center, watching
- increase the light to dispel darkness
- make a workbench for someone
- bring a plant to work for everyone to enjoy
- give yourself opportunities to replenish yourself
- meditate on emptiness
- reduce clutter and complexity by giving away seldom-used possessions

- don't take a bad mood too seriously
- learn to ride the waves of thought
- discover how special you are
- choose how you react
- we don't have to forgive people if we don't judge them in the first place
- massage your scalp with essential oils
- learn from obstacles placed on the path
- read about points of view that differ from your own
- do not try to make something out of everything
- share a banana split
- spruce up the house here and there
- shower someone who is ill with positive thoughts
- cultivate relationships with those who can teach you
- make grilled cheese sandwiches and tomato soup
- write down ten practical and then ten impractical things you'd like to do right now that would give you pleasure

- set a goal to understand yourself
- use a stationary bike or treadmill when you cannot exercise outside
- take care of tiny little details
- hear the sounds around you
- listen to inspirational or educational tapes in the car
- don't make anyone the butt of your humor
- nip stress in the bud
- campaign for closed captioning
- know when to call it quits
- thank the cockpit crew at the end of the flight
- once you have a clear vision of the right thing to do, start acting on it
- sneak in some abdominal crunches and stretching every day
- live your life like a competent captain: set a course and steer your boat when necessary, but let the wind and waves do most of the work

- to have no likes or dislikes is supreme attainment of equanimity
- if you ride a bus, wish the driver a good day
- organize all of the closets
- have a romantic message posted on a scoreboard
- beliefs become self-fulfilling prophecies
- surprise family members by putting a chocolate mint on each pillow
- stay aware of your moment-to-moment experience
- soften and be merciful
- give plants food when they need it
- bring awareness to the task of cleaning up
- write a note of appreciation to one of your favorite teachers about the difference he or she made in your life
- promote good in others
- bring a plate of cookies or a pot of stew to a new neighbor

- surrender to what is
- chalk a poem on the sidewalk
- be true to yourself
- your worst enemy cannot harm you as much as your own thoughts
- master your moods
- return books before they are overdue
- your experience is what you do with what happens to you
- drive your car less
- be calm in the face of someone else's hysteria
- ask, what can I let go of right now?
- tell someone how great they look
- give heart to those who are low
- gain strength from your loved ones
- do frequent self-examinations
- to the extent that you control your thoughts, you control your world

- cleanse the energy in the bedroom several times a year
- give thought to the future effects of present deeds
- eat before you go to the supermarket
- acknowledge your weaknesses
- exercise at your own pace; it should be exhilarating, not painful
- send a note of praise to a great coworker
- allow your mind to solve a problem while you are busy doing something else
- celebrate this moment
- act with good intentions
- release all suffering
- live life right now
- remind yourself that everything you do, think, and dream matters
- spend hours in a library for pleasure
- if our inner household is not in order, no outer household will be in order

- base your expectations on reality
- wake up!
- If you care enough for the result, you will almost always attain it (William James)
- throw out a bad memory
- reduce work stress by cultivating calmness and awareness in the work domain
- let mindfulness guide your actions
- eliminate the obsession with getting everything done — almost everything can wait
- be nice to your brothers and sisters
- say hello to strangers
- think for yourself
- examine any subject that arouses curiosity
- remember that you can always learn
- He who knows he has enough is rich (Lao-tzu)
- choose carefully: what you choose could determine what you become

- teach kids to use their creativity
- walk the dog on a new route
- move on
- go to bed at a regular hour every night
- see challenges from new angles
- get away from your desk at lunchtime
- direct your future
- practice yoga before breakfast
- read to someone
- leave the table with a little room in your stomach
- join Teach America
- in winter, sip warm or hot water with lemon
- buy lunch for a coworker
- sing with children
- learn outside the lines
- relieve a child's problem
- help disadvantaged children find a reason to laugh
- take quiet time every day

- don't engage in fault finding
- concentrate on doing the best you can do
- in laughter, we transcend our predicaments
- take a step outside yourself
- take time to arrange a bouquet of flowers
- offer nourishment
- make it a point to be happy where you are
- accept others for who they are
- permit playfulness
- journey straight ahead, free of any encumbrance
- if you know someone has had a bad day, take him out for coffee or dinner
- your angry behavior reflects on you long after the anger has passed
- tell a young person you like what she's wearing
- practice good hygiene
- write funny captions on pictures in magazines and newspapers for others in your home to see

- show affection
- wear clothing made of natural fabrics
- be curious about what is happening in your body
- throw a celebration breakfast for someone
- shop at garage sales
- you can only have bliss if you don't chase it
- take someone on a surprise outing
- keep your spine neutral for good posture
- wherever you go from here is up to you
- detach yourself from everything that constricts you
- give family members "kindness coupons" they can redeem for special favors
- relax and clear your mind with a warm shower
- make a list of things that have been bugging you; change what you can and forget the rest
- let bad news in the right ear and out the left ear
- be present: recognize the signs of distraction and gently bring your mind back to the moment

- don't listen to the radio or TV when you cook
- reconcile two enemies
- say no to something so that you can make room for something more important
- celebrate your life and liberty, and pursue happiness
- leave some things unsaid
- do not fill up time just to fill it up
- make a house into a home
- do not be tossed around by every new idea
- encourage your children
- meditate on your third eye point (the sixth chakra) to help control your emotions
- never postpone a good deed you can do now
- carry a cup of coffee out to the porch for someone to enjoy in the morning sunshine
- drive as you wish your kids would drive
- write a fan letter to your favorite living author
- take the time to have a friend

- seek nothing
- thrive on affirmation and praise, but don't rely on it
- don't get stuck — do something!
- stop taking things personally
- believe in miracles
- remember that good things come from good habits
- be intellectually adventurous
- begin something brand-new today
- changing your behavior patterns actually creates new dendrites (nerve cell connections) in your brain
- let teenagers know that they are liked
- learn to have fun on your own
- practice telling and hearing the truth
- put relationships before rules
- plant a tree for baby's birthday
- learn what you can live without
- put on your favorite CD and dance
- read the best books first

- are you treating yourself with enough tenderness?
- pay your taxes on time
- for a long life, keep fish in multiples of nine
- build friendship between generations
- when shopping for groceries, spend most of your time on the perimeter of the store — in the fruit, vegetable, meat, and dairy departments
- teach life skills to kids
- sample a simpler life
- volunteer as a docent
- in the beginner's mind, there are many possibilities
- most mountain peaks can be scaled if you have the will, the strength, and the equipment to climb them
- make a list of ways to bring more kindness into the world
- if you are cooking or baking, make a little extra for a busy single mother
- recycle mail-order catalogs

- visit national monuments
- spend a weekend on a retreat
- do-it or fix-it yourself
- don't be restricted by your past experiences
- stop apologizing
- talk to the locals wherever you go
- streamline and downsize
- show respect for others' time
- let your unconscious mind work out a worry
- carry your own luggage
- transform negative thoughts
- enjoy your garden
- eat raw dishes more often
- apply creative solutions to real-life problems
- exercise discretion
- buy a set of postcards at a museum to bring the experience to someone who could not go
- affirm all the good things about yourself

- vote for politicians who make the environment part of their agenda
- when your blood sugar dives, breathe in lavender, rosemary, or both
- read a writing style and usage manual
- consciously decide to want less
- wait until one meal is digested before eating the next
- use your life wisely
- be polite under pressure
- do absolutely nothing for a while
- believe that others are doing the best they can
- clean with water and baking soda
- Zen gardening serves as a means of contemplation
- sometimes go along with what your partner or friend wants
- offer a healing touch, a healing word
- think good thoughts and they will become good deeds
- serve your mate chicken soup when he or she is sick

- **start every day a little happier**
- walk slowly
- inspire yourself
- distract yourself from an urge and let it pass
- the most important pose in your yoga practice is the Corpse/Relaxation Pose (*shavasana*)
- keep active files within reach
- get caught up in the romantic atmosphere of a wedding
- endow a teaching chair at your alma mater
- be grateful when you're feeling good
- leave a note on your child's pillow when you go out for the evening
- improve
- become mindful
- ask your spouse for a slow dance
- let go of bad habits
- sit in the grass

- pray under a cathedral of trees
- give a guy professional race-car driving lessons
- practice patience and nurturing through gardening
- respect quality
- read goofy joke books
- give as much as you take in your relationships
- reward yourself for every goal achieved
- try to rely on fewer gadgets
- the less you need, the freer you become
- negotiate peacefully
- how often do you wait to get through something just to move on to the next thing?
- relax deeply
- take your vitamins
- eat slowly and chew each bite ten times; work your way up to fifty
- play music when you're alone
- offer to vacuum Mom or Dad's car

- get into the habit of looking into the far distance, middle distance, and spaces in between
- persuade a smoker to quit
- if you cannot find the circumstances you want, make them
- motivate employees
- disturb natural flora and fauna as little as possible
- go out of your way to help a grandparent
- spend today bringing happiness to your friends and family
- don't try to win the argument; just listen to it
- learn to swim at the YMCA
- be an explorer
- say a peace prayer
- sing a lullaby
- take a child to the park to feed the ducks
- be the eyes and ears for a friend who is looking for something related to an interest or hobby

- if you love your enemies, you will have no enemies
- look people in the eye when you talk to them
- put a love note in your mate's cosmetic or shaving kit before a trip
- find safe, easy chores for young children
- help others achieve their dreams
- do not cause suffering to another
- share
- Live in each season as it passes; and resign yourself to the influences of each (Henry David Thoreau)
- open yourself to what is beautiful and good
- revel in the luxury of being alive
- inspire others to be happy
- do everything with love
- if you give, you will be provided for
- think things through
- walk a dog
- accept your fear and anger and then let it go

- hang a heart from your child's doorway as a good-morning surprise
- be willing to change your mind
- do something generous
- use words with the greatest care
- call a politician on the carpet for empty promises
- be a fun person: good appetite, interesting work, good storyteller, slightly twisted humor, fresh insight, brave choices
- congratulate yourself every time you successfully reduce your anger and control your behavior
- pay attention to what you are eating
- give happily
- get rid of objects that weigh you down
- enjoy a music festival
- the more you learn, the more you improve your ability to learn
- rent a funny movie

- be patient with the finicky eater in your family
- take a second honeymoon
- bring more order to life
- don't talk about anyone who is not present
- lower your intake of bread, pasta, and pizza
- give your parents theater tickets for two
- in spring, meditate on the new life that is blossoming
- don't blame anyone — including yourself — for life's disappointments
- when you feel yourself getting angry, breathe for at least ten counts
- if you see yourself as living in a universe of plenty, you will be more willing to share
- campaign to have unjust laws changed
- keep only three small plants in the bedroom to promote health, harmony, and well-being
- shovel snow off someone else's driveway
- hold your child's hand every chance you get

- control your reactions
- don't fill your mind with poisonous thoughts
- take a spring break like the one you had in school
- give a child a colored pencil kit
- unsubscribe to magazines you no longer read
- try to create a garden that looks and feels natural
- be inspired by others' excellence
- get your life organized   but not too organized
- by sheer determination, you can improve your mind
- go to children's museums
- listen to what other people want without reacting, objecting, arguing, fighting, or resisting
- be too confident for worry, too noble for anger, too strong for fear
- encourage your mate to take time out with friends
- try not to defend yourself
- share your book-of-the-moment by buying a copy for someone

 instant karma

- grow things to eat
- try making one new meal each week
- keep your words gentle, loving, accurate, and positive
- repair a child's old teddy bear
- shop at farmers' markets
- donate secondhand books
- serve someone tea
- use every means throughout the day to guard your *samadhi*—power—just as you would protect a child
- strive to achieve whatever you think you cannot
- respect your children's privacy
- give for the sake of giving
- accept that life changes constantly
- change the next moment by breaking the pattern and doing something different
- make challah bread for Shabbat
- be truly present
- make story time special for kids

- make peace of mind your priority
- pay homage to war veterans
- life is about the journey, not the destination
- listen carefully to what is meant, not just what is said
- never discourage a child's individuality
- love yourself first
- pack a picnic and take your family on a trip to the country
- take children horseback riding
- each step is a place to learn
- celebrate a bill of good health from the doctor
- teach someone how to use a computer
- be present for your partner
- make conscious choices about how you spend your time
- let go of anger
- compassion is based on knowing that all human beings have the same innate desire to be happy

- take ice cream to a sick friend
- create an affirmation for each of your life areas
- It is by studying little things that we attain the great art of having as little misery and as much happiness as possible (Samuel Johnson)
- become a teacher in an adult education program
- tape a positive message to the bathroom mirror, refrigerator, and computer monitor
- pass down a special recipe
- declare a moratorium on spending money
- let everyone sleep late on a Sunday morning
- accept criticism gracefully
- reward yourself
- remember that all things pass
- forget the number on the bathroom scale
- take your grandchildren along on a trip
- volunteer to run errands for someone who can't make the trip

- listen to your favorite music while ironing
- do the work for yourself
- help the disabled through mental or physical therapy, companionship, and advocacy
- donate your favorite toys to a day-care center
- learn to find meaning in the joys that fade
- feel comfortable as a completely ordinary person
- tip the band members at concerts in the park
- learn to let go
- volunteer to lead a youth group
- share your French fries
- ignore infomercials
- explore a city at a browser's pace
- do someone's Saturday chores
- give good, accurate directions
- whenever walking in *kinhin* (walking meditation), keep your mind totally focused on your environment, not on the thoughts that distract you

- focus on what you hope to accomplish
- strive to live a simpler life
- give the gift of good cheer
- direct your eye inward
- take frequent breaks
- consume fewer goods
- create thoughts that will weaken or destroy a bad thought
- pick out one thing you did well for the day and congratulate yourself
- cancel all but one or two of your credit cards
- acknowledge your anger and fear
- try to put what you learn into practice in your daily life
- for greater lung capacity, push as much air out as you can before inhaling
- be sincere
- be indifferent to what others may think or say
- walk dogs for an animal shelter

- share your love, your wisdom, and your wealth
- recognize religion as something personal
- protect robin's eggs
- avoid unnecessary pain
- experience the present moment without reminiscences, comparisons, evaluations, judgments
- promote safe schools
- offer to plant and maintain an elderly person's flower garden
- look at something and say, "yes, I can make it better"
- exercise every day
- in the morning, brush your teeth and gums; scrape your tongue
- give your least favorite food another chance
- get extra rest when you need it
- open your eyes a little more
- try to see things as they really are rather than allowing problems to be distorted or magnified by worry

- find the fun parts
- finish what you start
- believe that the good in a human being will be revealed to you
- recite the formal Buddhist refuge vows: "in the Buddha, in the dharma, in the sangha"
- never resist a generous impulse
- speak and act with loving-kindness
- buy flowers for your home on Fridays
- start everything with acceptance
- the next time you feel the urge to criticize, stop yourself
- try positive hypnosis
- broaden someone's horizons
- build in extra time to walk during errands
- bring someone lemonade on a very hot day
- challenge accepted assumptions before reaching a conclusion

- graduate from college
- host a foreign exchange student
- be a leader
- convert to geothermal energy
- start a greenhouse, especially in the winter
- point out the good qualities in other people
- send an unexpected letter to an old friend
- kick the potato habit
- spend money consciously and with joy
- follow your heart
- let go of your need to control and learn to trust
- feel an intimate connection with earth
- provide a home where children can be children
- keep life in your house — live creatures and plants bring in energy
- supervise your children's television viewing habits
- don't take your friends for granted
- come up with ideas for others

- accept people regardless of their social station
- always patch things up with friends
- slip a dollar into your child's pocket
- play soft music
- wake up fifteen minutes early for a spiritual practice
- let go of reason's grip from time to time
- return again to the breath
- attend to little things before they get bigger
- only you can make you happy
- precision learned in Pilates affects how you walk into a room, how you sit, how you carry yourself through life
- help children by volunteering at a recreation program
- engage in activities that give you joy
- transfer your meditation practice into everyday life
- help others
- equip the family cars with first-aid kits
- radiate energy
- earn the trust of those around you

- look inward for some part of each day
- enjoy the smell of grass and foliage along your bicycle path
- make a photo calendar to give grandparents for the new year
- We are free to be at peace with ourselves and others, and also with nature (Thomas Merton)
- do seated breath stretches: breathe into your front, then into your back, then into each side
- use discretion
- consume less caffeine and meditation will become easier
- refresh a weary traveler
- get enough sleep, exercise, and healthy food
- approach life with a Zen attitude
- do not underrate your own abilities
- help a friend without being asked
- turn on the TV with awareness

- when washing your own car, offer to wash someone else's
- promote uncompromising vision
- don't covet the possessions of others
- meditation is learning to focus and concentrate on the smallest acts of daily life
- aim for self-mastery
- get your endorphins pumping
- recycle
- have pizza delivered to your employees when they work late
- take control of the controls
- live each day for itself
- mend your broken heart
- donate vegetables from your garden to the local soup kitchen
- eat only when relaxed
- have a realistic time frame for your dreams

- befriending silence is a process of learning to befriend ourselves
- make snow angels
- include children in family activity decisions
- give easy to follow instructions
- find something you are gung-ho about
- when you like someone, tell them
- clean your house with nontoxic products
- write friendship poems
- turn out a light for someone who can't reach the switch
- act for the greater good
- reupholster your favorite chair
- try to keep your mouth shut when you notice you have a strong desire to be right
- avoid eating for at least two hours before bedtime
- too many plants, which give off yang energy, can disturb one's sleep

- make Sunday dinner special
- lighten the burden of another
- read the newspaper together on Sunday morning
- pay much closer attention
- use books to help you find meaning, if not answers
- believe that you can make an impact
- keep quiet if you can't say anything nice
- what you do today is what matters most
- move on: life is too valuable to get stuck
- a good mind, a good heart, warm feelings —
  these are the most important things
- leave work at work when you go on vacation
- breathe through your nose
- give a child a new box of crayons
- use guilt to align your behavior with your
  consciousness, then let go of the guilt
- be gentle with yourself, but firm with your
  expectations

- take a spending break for thirty days
- speak slowly, calmly, quietly, clearly, and with confidence
- the next time you stay in a hotel, leave a generous tip in an envelope addressed "Maid"
- experience the sacred in every moment
- savor the fleeting delights of the day
- want nothing
- do pelvic rotations while sitting cross-legged to address the second chakra
- watch educational television
- when you're angry with someone, try to remember something nice that person has said or done
- shift to a diet of natural, healthy, and simple food — away from highly processed foods, meat, and sugar
- meditate on light
- work hard (but not too hard)
- use energy-efficient lightbulbs

- campaign to overhaul the child welfare system
- the freedom to choose and change belongs to you
- volunteer to answer phones for a suicide hotline
- waste time on the spur of the moment
- focus on your meals—the colors, flavors, textures, temperature
- don't try to plan every minute of your day
- promote the spirit of Christmas all year long
- correct your mistakes
- learn about other cultures
- let go of every mental habit that holds you back
- be a browser, not a buyer
- donate to charity and thrift shops
- get out of your head by walking
- reassure kids when they are scared
- let yourself feel things
- whenever you are in a negative frame of mind, think of ten things you are grateful for

- take your mentor out to lunch
- support banning all weapons
- practice letting go of feeling not good enough
- accept what you can't change; change what you can
- help beautify your town
- see the nurturing aspects of daily living
- as a leader, provide incentives and rewards
- chew your food slowly so you can savor all the flavors
- visualization can reframe a warped self-portrait
- really enjoy your vacation
- make up food baskets for needy families
  at Thanksgiving and Christmas
- wash dishes by hand
- help someone take advantage of an opportunity
- believe that what others say is what they mean
- give to the blood bank
- start something today
- react constructively

- give another driver the parking space you spotted first
- donate to neighbors who collect for good causes
- help make the world safe for children
- aim and swing for the fence
- audition for a community play
- be kind to a pushy salesperson
- require children to take responsibility for their actions
- enjoy leisurely evenings, uninterrupted by TV
- save a penny to earn a penny
- react to unpleasantness with calm and equanimity
- spend at least twenty minutes a day outside in the fresh air
- be kinder than necessary
- hold positive thoughts in your mind
- seek without seeking: sit still, clear your mind, wait
- open yourself to the way your life is rather than how you imagine it should be
- the Tao's principle is spontaneity

- ask, will this so-called convenience really simplify my life?
- treat yourself to dinner at a very nice restaurant
- stop worrying
- eliminate the irrelevant
- take a bag of sandwiches to the local homeless shelter
- soak in a hot bath before going to bed
- practice loving-kindness
- go for a country drive with a loved one
- get to work early
- if there is a gulf, start building a bridge
- make banana splits for your child and your child's friends
- well-spoken words bear fruit in one who puts them into practice
- see everything you do as a piece of art
- listen empathetically
- sip warm water with your meal

- grow deep
- the more you give, the wealthier you become
- eliminate ten things from your life
- take a we-try-harder approach to service
- work with what you have
- hold yourself to the highest standards
- bring up children who behave in public
- experience the length of breath
- live with a consciousness of your mortality
- acceptance produces a resilient mind
- say something nice to someone
- celebrate being alive
- pay attention to your Freudian slips
- kick off your shoes and splash your feet in a fountain
- if your heart is large with understanding and compassion, a word or deed will not have the power to make you suffer
- help your children grow up

- give help, not advice
- accomplish something every day
- find things to be happy about on your own
- send a letter of appreciation to a public servant
- express support for someone else's personal project
- don't resort to sarcasm
- feel deserving of happiness
- gain control over your automatic responses
- lift weights for exercise
- start each day with kisses
- make a daily list of things to do
- pull some weeds in your neighborhood
- eliminate your bad habits one by one
- entertain yourself
- evolve
- become a more thoughtful friend
- meditate at least twenty minutes; progress to sixty minutes

- strap a pillow on the behind of a rookie roller-skater
- living Zen means you have no future — right now is your only life; make it count for everything
- find a use for everything
- say, "May all beings be awake, may all beings be happy, may all beings be at peace"
- do your inner work every day
- find the truth right where you are
- shake a child's hand in greeting
- silence is a refuge and a teacher
- bring fresh-picked flowers to the fire station
- help a child learn geography
- look at all the details of a leaf or rock in the sunshine
- If one advances confidently in the direction of his dreams, he will meet with a success unexpected in common hours (Henry David Thoreau)
- delight at the prospect of a new day
- temper your take-out restaurant habit

- give gifts often for permanent wooing
- use careful speech
- save habitats for all beings
- help invent jobs for the millennium
- prepare a "Bad Day Survival Kit" full of things that give you confidence
- give up your seat for someone else
- life is how you see it
- learn yoga poses that open and release your chakras and flood them with *prana,* or life energy
- keep a list of new words you read or hear and review them until they become part of your vocabulary
- give someone a funny "Get Well" card
- do everything with enthusiasm
- make a birthday banner for someone
- travel your own road
- take no notice of those who laugh at your spiritual path
- calm your desires

- realize that you are not your bad habit
- turn the other cheek
- make food for others
- offer to pay for someone behind you in line
- reduce your debt
- help out at your child's school
- take someone out for coffee or ice cream
- be tender with the young
- insulate and weatherproof your house
- don't live like a robot
- foil your own expectations!
- in Corpse Pose, concentrate on quieting the breath, focusing on its rhythm
- clean up the bathroom after yourself
- respect the intelligence and motives of others
- love completely and unselfishly
- offer milk and graham crackers to someone feeling down

- cast compliments, not aspersions
- hang cut-lead crystals in your windows to bring energy into the home
- inspire others
- envision and create
- don't force the issue
- say a prayer of thanks on Thanksgiving
- vote for a deserving candidate
- do the impossible
- buy a box of Valentine's Day cards and use them throughout the year for your sweetheart and family
- get ahead in your work
- develop the talents you have inherited
- listen to another person's stories
- practice being brave
- plan your meals to include plant-based foods
- walk a path as quietly as possible
- be content to satisfy basic needs only

- make happiness a factor in decision-making
- listen to people telling stories about their childhood
- demonstrate care through touch or words
- create a Zen ritual
- analyze what kind of thoughts your mind produces
- plan adventure activities
- submit a suggestion that saves money for your company
- ask for peace of mind
- never dramatize a difficulty
- return everything you have borrowed
- complain less and listen more
- view struggles as growth opportunities
- just be there
- clarify your thoughts and desires
- after you have given your opinion, withdraw, and don't concern yourself with the outcome
- teach an adult to read

- erase any negative messages on your "internal tape"
- make a Dairy Queen run late at night
- never compare yourself with others
- there is always a piece of fortune in misfortune
- learn tai chi animal walks for balance and body awareness
- dharma enables us to integrate the many diverse experiences of life into a meaningful, coherent whole
- fashion your life the way an artist creates a great work of art
- take small actions every day to advance your dreams
- examine your true worth
- be your spouse's best friend
- read four dictionary pages a day
- it takes courage to grow up and turn out to be who you really are (e.e. cummings)
- if you want to become full, let yourself be empty
- yoga is about self-acceptance, not self-improvement

- display ribbons and trophies won by a youngster
- send clear signals
- rent *Pollyanna*
- volunteer to raise a Seeing Eye dog until it is ready to be trained
- consider the true cost of acquiring something new
- become aware of your breathing once an hour
- entertain a child
- take a walk during your lunch hour
- reduce meaningless activity
- share without hesitation when others are in need
- help your spouse get eight hours of sleep
- wake up and say, "I would like to make a difference in the world today"
- work through things step-by-step, one day at a time
- make an extra effort
- nurture the good feelings in your relationships
- use positive thinking to help you achieve your goals

- help a child prepare for a spelling bee
- get through a day without excuses
- eat all your spinach
- reclaim your weekend; don't leave all your errands for Saturday
- explore your unconscious
- start over
- apologize to your child when you're at fault
- don't offer unwanted help
- keep basic supplies on hand
- appreciate accomplished musicians
- change the way you think about yourself
- get an early start
- have a loving relationship with your spouse
- teach your children the value of money
- accept what your loved ones can and can't give
- strengthen the quadriceps by practicing the Proud Warrior yoga position

- establish a calming routine that you can use if you feel yourself getting angry
- put a flower on someone's pillow
- know your options
- replace youth with mystery
- settle on a park bench, close your eyes, and take in what happens around you
- donate canned goods
- plant a windowbox with flowers
- fall in love with a homeless kitty
- eat three meals a day
- for one week, bring no harm in thought, word, or deed to any living creature
- avoid using electric blankets
- be less harsh with yourself and with others
- be enthusiastic about something
- swim with life's currents, not against them
- keep a journal of compliments given to your child

- hide treat coupons for others to find
- give money to those who need it
- find pleasure in your deference
- stretch throughout the day
- stamp out conformity
- deliver more than you are getting paid to do
- for serenity, put a statue of Buddha in your house
- learn the true meaning of the holidays
- be mindful of what you're doing and why
- your character is your destiny
- avoid hot, spicy, or pungent foods
- temporary solitude is necessary for the soul
- start a conversation
- move beyond the self
- refuse to lie, gossip, or inflame people
- when you walk, just walk
- set the coffeepot to turn on in the morning for sleepyheads

- realize that not everything needs to be done today
- take a kid to the zoo
- get a group together to make crib quilts for ICU babies in the hospital
- use five free minutes to start a project
- always be content with whatever happens
- stop trying to control
- when you give a gift, don't expect anything in return
- keep your thoughts in a journal
- do simple yoga poses with your kids
- sometimes not getting what you want is the best thing for you
- associate with positive people
- be social
- face a limitation and give your very best
- don't play favorites
- if it's raining outside, have a picnic on the living room floor

- write a postcard to someone you're thinking about
- love is best when it is not out of desperation
- applaud people who are practicing
- most things can wait
- fix gourmet meals
- let someone go in front of you at the coffee shop
- let go of misery
- don't recline your seat in a crowded airplane
- answer e-mails promptly
- look for the helping message in your dreams
- identify your bad habit triggers as well as the root of the bad habit
- take baby steps to get through the difficult days
- don't ignore hunches
- when you become more calm and serene on the inside, the world becomes more calm and serene on the outside
- be a creative cook

- do the yoga Lying Spinal Twist to loosen a tight back and torso muscles
- avoid caffeine in the afternoon
- propose a toast
- be aware of difficulties but believe they can be overcome
- use moderation
- feel worthy of abundance
- your consciousness radiates out even further than your imagination
- let go of past sorrows as well as anxieties about the future
- appreciate athletes' hard work
- let go of desire
- don't over-analyze
- send your spouse a valentine on the 14th of every month
- if you don't understand, ask

- maintain courtesy at all times
- thank the referees at the end of a game — even if your team lost
- burn incense to help calm the mind when you meditate
- learn orienteering
- find compassionate alternatives
- teach by example
- look for contentment from within
- hunt for seashells
- do nothing to excess
- keep field glasses and a bird book by the window
- conserve water
- join a health food co-op
- cook someone's favorite meal on his or her birthday
- stop fidgeting and nail biting
- make someone laugh
- exercise consistently

- have patience
- create peace in your own life
- volunteer at a zoo
- mind your own business
- practice yoga to tone your muscles, trim excess weight, and experience boundless energy
- let go of pain, fear, and insecurity
- make your heart as open as the sky
- tell your child a bedtime story
- control your material desires
- don't plan the future by the past
- take time for heart-to-heart chats
- eat slowly and savor the moment
- fill someone's gas tank for him or her
- read books of every religion
- do the yoga Tree Pose to improve balance and poise
- stay centered when things are out of balance
- keep a homeowner's journal and project planner

- work with integrity
- practice goodness
- let each breath clear your mind and open your heart
- share a special poem with your child
- always expect the best and be prepared for the worst
- have an open mind
- good deeds are immortal
- have a family photo enlarged and send it to a grandparent
- love nature
- give confidence to others
- confide in someone
- ask yourself, am I paying attention?
- be good for something
- choose to become better
- celebrate Be Kind to Animals Week
- read a spiritual passage, then give yourself time to consider it

- absorb information slowly
- develop discipline by deliberately and daily forcing yourself to do something nonessential
- tie up loose ends
- immerse yourself in all there is to see, hear, and smell right now
- put a treasure in someone's pocket
- eat foods that are in season
- take a grandparent's dog for a walk
- serve your country
- be yourself
- plan your family
- learn from your anger
- weigh the advantages of forgiveness and resentment — then choose
- increase yin by doing stretching exercises like yoga and tai chi, meditating in the evening, staying up late, and spending a lot of time indoors

- study philosophers who have a positive outlook on life
- turn a business trip into an adventure
- listen for the sake of listening
- send a week's worth of birthday cards to someone special
- be at the airport waiting for a loved one
- focus less on calories and fat, more on exercise
- listen to the leaves in autumn
- let go of old hurts and angers
- be certain that your motivation is love, not fear
- have a passion for excellence
- stand up straighter
- sit up in front instead of in the back
- what are you doing for others?
- roll up your sleeves and work hard
- whether you win or lose, be nice to the opposition
- leave everyone laughing
- start a box for donations to a local charity

- regard food as medicine to sustain health and ward off illness
- factor in downtime: free time, transition time, time doing nothing
- vacation at a cooking school
- ask for help
- don't worry that you won't get it all done
- teach someone how to use a thesaurus
- it is better to conquer yourself than to conquer thousands of others
- ask a child to sing you a song
- aid the sick — through hospitals, the Red Cross, or hospice care
- earn the respect of your employer
- Zen means doing ordinary things willfully and cheerfully (Reginald H. Blyth)
- when you bring in something new, throw out something old

- buy a supply of paper plates and take a week's vacation from dishwashing
- be money smart
- support the National Register of Historic Places
- attend to each moment and learn something new
- invest time in fulfilling your dreams
- be an apprentice
- introduce variety into your diet
- explore your goals in career, finances, home, spirituality, health, fun, travel, and education
- cultivate contentment
- make a quiet corner for your child
- express gladness in tangible ways
- occupy yourself with living life, not just talking about it
- conflict is inevitable, fighting is optional
- before purchasing something, try the 30-day test: write down what you want, and ask yourself in 30 days if you still want or need it

- look with curiosity
- forgive someone's mean-spirited act
- keep a daily mood journal
- seek out and talk to someone who does what you want to do most
- say prayers for guidance and divine wisdom
- get out of your own way
- spend a weekend in a cozy cabin in the woods with no phones or television
- show restraint when necessary
- every grocery shopping trip, buy a can of vegetables or bag of grain to donate to a hunger program
- neither grasp at delights nor reject the repulsive
- rest when exhausted
- define yourself by who you are instead of by what you do
- develop some common interests with loved ones
- put candy hearts in someone's lunch box

- complete the tasks on your daily to-do list
- learn only those things that you really need and want to know
- drink tea in mindfulness
- appreciate the silence of close friendship
- reduce your meat consumption
- share with your family the news of your life
- criticize less and compliment more
- build a birdhouse
- explore, take chances, be adventurous
- carry heavy things for the elderly or disabled
- schedule a family reading hour
- give regular hugs and kisses
- look at all of your knowledge as a gift
- the more generous you are, the more loving-kindness you cultivate
- donate used games to a senior citizen center
- get to know the morning waitress

 instant karma

- let others do things their own way
- eat foods that are cooling in the spring
- don't worry about who gets the credit
- never eat lunch at your desk
- let go of wanting, and experience freedom
- don't procrastinate
- talk when necessary
- read something for pleasure
- hang a May basket on someone's doorknob
- the more we forget about our own egos, the more open we are to love
- lend an ear
- strive for moderation in all things
- be a godparent to a friend's child
- try to lift someone else's gloom
- commit to orderliness
- love your partner
- read Sir Thomas More's writings

- lighten up
- be aware of your own achievements
- feel your breath in your nostrils
- let someone sleep
- learn the difference between being hungry and thinking you are hungry
- pare down portions and share your food
- observe your child in the classroom to understand that part of his or her life
- show respect
- honor your teachers
- ask, what have I always wanted to do that I have never done? and then try it
- serenade your beloved
- be comfortable in your own skin
- be courageous
- have faith
- make sacrifices to attain great happiness

- widen your reading horizons
- try eating a spicy meal to quell nervousness
- leave gaps in your calendar for spontaneity
- teach your children how to love and to empathize
- appreciate and honor the beauty in life
- say a daily prayer
- get some dirt under your fingernails
- start a savings account
- enjoy the anticipation of heading home
- shape up your abdominals
- consider getting rid of everything you own and starting over
- purchase nontoxic cleaning agents
- reduce your needs for goods and services
- when you change your attitudes, you can change your behaviors, and thus change your karma
- accept forgiveness from others
- cut back on caffeine

- ride your bike to work
- put a cherry on top of a kid's dessert
- make your health a priority
- encourage your children to donate unused toys to less fortunate children
- look for joy in the least obvious places
- be the person who makes a new pot of coffee at the office
- try the healing breath pattern called "dog breath" that is just like a dog's rapid panting
- be grateful to those who make you happy
- watch
- get involved in a worthwhile project
- buy the wine or cheese that your partner likes
- have respect for others' faith
- the 1,000-mile journey begins with a single step
- when nothing is yours, no one can take anything from you

- believe that you are the best person for the job
- take instruction on *kapalabhati,* the cleansing breath
- don't treat your lawn with chemicals
- patronize the local hardware store
- say no politely
- learn how to store food to retain its *chi*
- use the solitude of meditation to help you learn everything
- remove your watch on weekends
- make time for yourself
- produce original work
- offer equal opportunity
- catch children being good
- always get back on the horse
- take walks daily
- neither hide nor display your life
- meet someone halfway
- partake in riddles, puzzles, and puns

- ask, is the problem the situation or is it my reaction to the situation?
- set aside time for spiritual study
- read *The Little Engine That Could* to children
- find tranquility in time alone
- view everyday surroundings with a tourist's eye
- carry on a long phone call with someone who needs it
- every single thing you do matters
- indulge your wanderlust and hit the road
- don't become frustrated by little setbacks
- allow for the possibilities
- recount your blessings every day
- let go of stress without analyzing it
- forget the Joneses
- overcome attachment and aversion, pride and fear, sorrow and grief
- take pictures of a bride and groom and enlarge them as a gift

- gratefulness makes the soul great
- accept irritations and frustrations with either humor or serenity
- carry something to read with you
- buy, cook, serve, and eat food in ways that demonstrate appreciation and care
- know how the government works
- give an off-the-cuff compliment
- clear away whatever doesn't ring true
- in moments of tension, remember to breathe
- be willing and able
- help kids expect the unexpected
- reside in the present
- still your protesting thoughts
- do not argue with your kids over their clothing styles
- encourage others to develop their strengths
- give the gift of peaceful surroundings
- coach a Little League team

- buy local produce and ingredients
- don't try to solve your problems when you are in a bad mood
- plan first, then act
- enjoy something when it presents itself, but don't crave it when it is not there
- waste nothing
- when you feel angry, do not say or do anything — just practice mindfulness
- eat anything in moderation
- appreciate your happy relationships and accept your imperfect relationships
- protect your family
- always be ready to find pleasure, but do not seek it
- become an organic gardener
- break a bad habit
- pay attention to what drives you to speak critically
- eat mindfully

- believe that every day is the best day of the year
- when you are rushing, consciously slow your pace
- apply a cold compress to someone's fevered brow
- calculate the possible consequences of an action before you act
- maintain a good sense of humor about your child's mistakes, as well as your own
- learn to become successful by listening to others' stories of personal triumphs
- give up the things that bind you
- appreciate 70 degree-F days
- use cloth bags instead of paper or plastic
- gracefully accept what the universe presents to you
- don't call your friends to recount every day's mundane minutiae
- find fun people
- be relaxed and flexible (yin) while maintaining a sense of focus and purpose (yang)

- avoid those who choose to do wrong
- surprise your mate every once in a while
- take a sibling to a Saturday matinee
- pay bills instead of paying interest
- extend invitations that include children
- become the moment
- put away enough money for retirement
- try not making any excuses for 24 hours
- unless you are sinless, do not talk about the sins of others
- satisfy your five senses
- realize that body, breath, and mind are one inseparable unit
- notice the silence between sounds
- be the kind of person who makes things happen
- show love with words, touch, thoughtfulness
- donate medical equipment to a hospital in the name of a loved one

- avoid things that you may become addicted to
- share a picture book with a preschooler
- your beliefs define your realities
- focus on that which you can control
- slow down
- recognize your connection to all animals
- make your compassion contagious
- from a standing *namaste* (prayer) position, extend arms up and back 60 degrees as you inhale; exhale and return to the starting position
- live your wisdom
- don't diet or binge
- let another driver merge into your lane
- tell people what they're doing right, not what they're doing wrong
- wipe off counters after you have used them
- buy an efficient automobile
- sandwich criticism between layers of praise

- think light
- achieve success, but without aggression or arrogance
- be content at work and at home
- redefine a problem as a test, and see if you can learn something from it
- find ways to make a kid feel big
- drop your defenses
- prepare an elegant tea service for grandparents
- learn to trust yourself
- go on a chilly jog around the park
- send flowers to express your love for someone
- rekindle friendships
- refrain from actions that cause suffering
- continually begin anew
- whatever you do, do it wholeheartedly
- moderate your reactions
- whatever system of spirituality you practice, do it every day

- learn how things are made and how things work
- ask directions
- if you are down, get moving
- let go of rigid ideas
- put people first
- focus on your connection with someone, not on what separates you
- find a fountain and make a wish
- give the gift of dharma — open up and talk with others about what is really meaningful
- maintain your composure under any circumstance
- lounge on the couch with your child and "hang out"
- exercise for fun
- explore someplace new
- give your teenager a calendar marked with family birthdays and anniversaries
- express love by listening
- send in a contribution to a magazine

- clean your home with natural products containing essential oils
- open yourself to all the support that is around you and in you
- every minute counts
- support gun control
- look beyond the obvious
- volunteer at a church or for a civic group
- be a good navigator for a driver
- fast for a weekend
- volunteer to work with children who have AIDS
- celebrate each thing you accomplish, no matter how small
- eat mainly "free-range" meats, and in moderation
- know where the fire exits are
- consume most of your calories earlier in the day and fewer calories later in the day
- know the minute details of your body

- take time for fireside chats
- say good-bye to an unhealthy habit
- give a gift certificate for a ballroom dancing class to a couple planning their wedding
- stop negativity in its tracks — take a deep breath and clear your mind
- balance your active and passive activities
- offer someone a mint
- write your spouse an "I'm so glad I married you" letter
- dedicate a song to someone on the radio
- improve your marriage continuously
- sometimes it's okay to give others what they want!
- refuse to engage in cruel, covetous, or otherwise nasty thoughts
- give honest answers
- stay happy and present and you'll have no reason to remember or repeat the past
- acquire a knack for calming people's fears

- in forgetting oneself, one is found
- view the world as if you were a child: play and create
- make room for mystery
- enjoy the physical aspects of your day: the softness of a coat, a shower after a brisk walk
- stand back from busyness
- release stress naturally — slow the heartbeat and improve air circulation — by using your diaphragm to breathe
- learn how to maintain things yourself
- is what you want to say an improvement over maintaining silence?
- rescue a hurt animal if you can do so safely
- go to watch all of someone's games
- dream it and do it
- let everything come and everything go
- read mythology or poetry for inspiration
- enjoy using your (clean) hands to prepare food

- buy an extra game for the bowlers in the next lane
- become more aware of what colors make you feel good
- pick up or return library books for someone
- acknowledge hardworking service people
- pick up litter anywhere you see it
- help stop drug abuse
- an open mind receives instruction, an open heart receives inspiration
- keep your sense of humor no matter what
- read the writings of Ralph Waldo Emerson
- don't wait for the perfect moment — it will never arrive
- do what you say you'll do
- get a better idea, not a bigger hammer
- do kind, peaceful things if you want your life to stand for peace and kindness
- express yourself at the right time, at the right place, with the right words, and the right attitude

- breathe in fatigue-fighting essential oils, such as rosemary or peppermint
- allow yoga to give strong emotions a gentle physical release by directing the attention to precise movement and accurate positioning
- suspend your need for attachment
- send handwritten letters that include photos, dried flowers, or quotes
- give homegrown vegetables to the local shelter
- share often and much
- give a senior citizen a gift certificate for a handyman visit
- don't take your spouse for granted
- imagine living your life without fear of expressing your dreams
- practice peaceful arts like yoga and tai chi
- replace some of the processed foods you eat with simpler, fresher, more natural foods

- drink water instead of alcohol
- be loyal
- ignore a rude remark
- when you travel, bring home small gifts for everyone
- leave a dollar bill where someone will discover it
- be flexible
- take a walk
- discover new insights
- move on from an unwinnable conflict
- bring two brown-bag lunches to a friend's house
- choose homemade food over fast food
- remember the worth of character
- select a meditation technique and stick with it
- take a few minutes each week to write a heartfelt letter
- let all of your thoughts become the teaching of the dharma
- save money for your "dream chair"
- take your spouse to a movie he will love

instant karma 144

- what you do for yourself you also do for others, and what you do for others you do for yourself
- let go of what you cannot change
- call someone and sing "Happy Birthday" on his or her special day
- be selfish when you need to be, without guilt
- send a love letter
- be informed
- read the directions
- have lots of books to read in case of bad weather
- be loving to those who do not love you
- cultivate a spirit of inquiry
- believe a person first and rumors last
- set a time each day for mantra practice
- appreciate intelligence and maturity
- observe clearly what you are experiencing and feeling
- make the subject as interesting as possible
- hold hands crossing the street

- go back to school
- curb hardheadedness
- celebrate ordinary days
- let an elderly person take a number before you at the deli
- avoid bandwagons
- arrive on time
- emphasize your family's strengths, not weaknesses
- take in an alley cat
- celebrate joy
- observe and experience without reacting
- read the editorials
- give money to help save Long Island Sound
- find a little privacy
- empower yourself
- when the day is over, let it go with good grace
- squeeze someone's arm, just for a moment, to let him or her know you care

- pay close attention to classroom instruction
- alternate activities
- stay fresh
- cuddle your children
- It is the greatest of all mistakes to do nothing because you can only do little. Do what you can. (Sydney Smith)
- sip hot water frequently throughout the day to dissolve *ama* (toxins) from your system
- don't be stubborn — offer a compromise
- find a healthy release
- be kind and respectful to teachers
- think of your life as an adult education class
- choose daily personal rituals: yoga, walk, meditation, etc.
- exercise to stimulate the heart and lungs, boost circulation, and deliver more oxygen to the brain
- give snakes the right-of-way
- plant wildflowers along roadsides

- wait for someone at the bus stop
- give a child who is going to sleepover camp a "write-home kit"
- let go of feeling incomplete or deprived
- practice eating mindfully, driving mindfully, taking out the garbage mindfully
- concentrate on loving thoughts — there are always people and things to love
- liven up your diet with ethnic cuisines
- help underprivileged kids on a regular basis
- lose yourself in something bigger than yourself
- note what is attractive and charming in others
- talk sweetly
- eat quality foods
- do tasks on your own
- double your joy by sharing it
- do backpacking meditation
- be loyal to your friends

- hang a picture of someone who has inspired you
- send a secret admirer card
- improve your muscle mass
- sit in a special spot near a window and read a favorite book
- be open and accessible
- improve the quality of your mental and physical life by practicing yoga
- keep as many options open as possible
- study the lives and works of your favorite artists
- if you realize that you have enough, you are truly rich
- allow your nature to express itself
- there is no substitute for paying attention!
- do not judge someone for being rude, unkind, or thoughtless
- meditate in a Zen garden
- be aware of the smells and sounds of a quiet time
- join a prison fellowship program

- keep your body pure and clean for the soul
  to reside in
- eat in balance with your way of life and your job
- walk with a loved one
- make a list of all the things you know how to do
- make things easier on yourself
- flexibility is freedom
- "adopt" a stream
- abandon disturbing thoughts
- include plenty of green, leafy vegetables in your diet
- in noting practice, you observe your experience with
  an attentive but relaxed mind, labeling sensations as
  they arise
- care for what you have
- find simple ways to make time for yourself
- help a child find unexpected ways of playing with
  household objects
- enjoy each small amusement

- put things back where you found them
- share your umbrella
- do daily creative-thinking exercises
- mist a room with a fine spray of spring water to neutralize negative energy
- make the most of what comes and the least of what goes
- find joy in generosity
- why waste energy being irritated by things you can't control?
- much of what happens to you is determined by your past karma, but how you react to it is very much within your freedom of the moment
- be supportive of someone's new endeavor
- let the outer chatter of the world pass you by
- watch less TV; read more books
- don't try to prove yourself to others
- have a custom calendar made from family snapshots

- don't say anything that is hurtful or untrue
- do one thing at a time
- watch your life unroll
- believe that you are lucky
- The individual becomes perfect when he loses his individuality in the all to which he belongs (D. T. Suzuki)
- volunteer to drive for Meals on Wheels
- stop chain letters
- put music in the air
- the awakened mind is free-flowing, natural, well-rounded
- memorize someone's favorite poem
- send someone you love a joke or a thought for the day
- act rather than react
- if you feel confused or bent out of shape — meditation is the way to straighten out
- avoid the temptation to sleep in on weekends

- keep only those things you use or love
- each day, tell someone that you like or appreciate something about them
- when you need to release excess energy — vacuum!
- don't rush
- enter someone's name in a sweepstakes
- provide paintboxes for needy children
- do small things with great love
- apologize to someone you offended
- be just as enthusiastic about the success of others as you are about your own
- choose the right moment to open your mouth
- mentally repeat the classic mantra *so hum* with your breath cycle
- Zen mind is waking up and living rather than going through the motions as if you were asleep
- make the waitstaff smile
- strive to have light in yourself

- explore the world through each of your senses
- read the morning newspaper outside
- write all those letters you've been meaning to write
- let go of territoriality
- protect life, practice generosity, behave responsibly, and consume mindfully
- try enjoying food simply as a source of sustenance
- go on a before-breakfast walk
- establish a daily meditation time
- photograph important events and milestones
- put someone's newspaper on his or her doorstep
- recognize each day as a gift
- whittle life down to 100 still-to-be-read books, a few pairs of jeans, some cotton shirts, and socks
- be a traveler instead of a tourist
- do things that make you feel passionately alive
- remember the needy at Christmas
- build white space into your calendar

- cultivate a voice that is easy to listen to
- avoid extremes
- keep quiet until you find out what you are thinking
- sit down and listen
- dry someone's wet shoes
- have a home where friends can easily congregate
- buy makeup from companies that sell cruelty-free products
- kiss Grandma's forehead
- laugh out loud
- steal a kiss from someone who is running out the door
- organize an in-home concert
- envelop yourself in a woolen blanket while reading
- do a core-strength workout several days per week
- buy a good dictionary
- like the people you work with
- if something makes you unhappy, try something else
- cook with someone you love

- approach life as if it were a banquet
- be part of a neighborhood watch group
- go to more dances
- fulfill your obligations
- put plants in the bathrooms
- manage your time by making lists
- put good dishes, silver, and linens into regular use
- cook a meal for yourself every day
- scrape the ice or snow off someone else's windshield
- discreetly remove your shoes under the restaurant table
- have a love story that is still being written
- thoroughly enjoy solitude
- remain calm — or learn how to become calm
- play with everything
- lasting happiness comes from deep respect for all beings and all life
- let a worry go

- hide a little surprise under the pillow
- let someone win at arm wrestling
- avoid sarcastic remarks
- get up and talk to someone — don't yell across rooms or to other floors
- keep mentally fit
- pass your life in peaceful serenity
- give admiring glances
- appreciate the pairing of food and wine
- concentrate on the solution rather than the problem
- avoid *rajasic* foods (very hot, bitter, sour, dry, salty) which promote agitation and discontentment
- establish a balance between what you have and what you want
- preserve life — even one insect, even one plant
- forgive yourself
- what matters is how well you live this short life and how well you learn to love

- surprise someone by cleaning his or her room
- give feedback and praise when you delegate responsibility
- age gracefully
- shed yourself of past identities
- show other people how to enjoy life
- use your time creatively
- thoughtful books make thoughtful gifts
- work on the things you can change
- settle for more
- view obstacles as opportunities
- find joy by giving it away
- release the creations of your imagination
- forgive yourself for any temporary failures
- create a seven-day healthy menu consisting of dishes that are quick and easy to shop for, prepare, and eat
- recognize your debt to others
- respect homemakers

- finish a degree
- be pure in your intentions
- share with loved ones
- take part in discovery and challenge
- get involved
- do not be a backseat driver
- send someone a friendship card
- keep the gleam in your eye
- consume less
- take your time completing whatever is undone
- don't think; see
- give sleep the attention it deserves
- plan a friendship ritual
- hire a string quartet to play for you and your mate at supper
- dedicate times at the beginning and end of the day to stillness
- be curious about life

- donate proceeds from a yard sale to a charitable organization
- have a constructive outlet for frustrations
- take pleasure in getting older
- ask forgiveness of all the people you have hurt
- place your desk or favorite chair to face the entrance to a room
- disagree without being disagreeable
- use your turn signal
- throw a get-acquainted party
- there is more to who you are than your body, intellect, and emotions
- plant a flower
- applaud former smokers for quitting
- believe in love at first sight
- hold hands during grace
- dharma practice is learning not to want or need things to be a certain way

- exercise without equipment
- time your routines to your personal rhythms
- know your abilities and strengths
- let go of minor annoyances before they become major conflicts
- Ask advice of him who governs himself well (Leonardo da Vinci)
- make or bake something for the church fair
- your view is only one perspective; why get so tied up in it?
- let go of regrets
- when you think you are hungry, try drinking water or green tea and see if your hunger abates
- keep moving forward
- when desire ends, there is peace
- allow others to have the glory
- learn about other cultures
- arrange a weekend trip with your spouse

- ride your bike more than you drive your car
- be kind to yourself
- bring crystals and semiprecious stones — earth — into your home
- practice Mountain Pose (simple standing pose) while waiting for the pasta to boil
- have a reputation for being gracious
- let sleeping dogs lie
- breathe deeply before you speak
- have dinner by candlelight at least once a week
- give to others for no reason
- make friends with animals you meet on your walks
- leave someone alone who is talking on the telephone
- leave something on your plate
- state affirmations in the present tense, as if they were already true
- improve literacy — through advocacy, tutoring, or mentoring

- wear clothes that don't chafe or bind
- rent yoga tapes and experiment with different types
- listen to the deep voice of a stream
- be your children's best teacher and coach
- focus on the real truth
- be willing to learn new things
- it is better to ask twice than lose your way once
- dine, don't eat
- give a child his or her first fishing pole
- give second chances
- support the high school band
- comfort someone afflicted by sorrow
- send love in letters and phone calls
- take one step forward
- dare to look lived-in
- use timesaving high-tech devices sparingly
- don't answer the phone just because it is ringing
- let go of feeling unworthy

- bounce on a small trampoline
- pause for a moment
- make a catnip mouse for a feline
- become a bigger human being
- make the best of your situation
- recognize the limitations of your body
- let the waiter tell you the daily specials
- mail letters or cards to family members for no reason
- confront prejudice whenever you hear it
- tell your parents you love them more often
- help a child overcome shyness
- value the moment
- appreciate everything you have
- appreciate things that are simple and ordinary and very real
- do not apologize for what you like to do
- kick off your shoes, roll up your pants, and wade into a creek

- read to the blind
- use bells with pleasant tinkling sounds to activate yang energy
- don't look to others for answers
- eat garden vegetables and pasta salad for lunch
- reread a book that made a difference in your life
- never question your happiness
- be punctual
- clean out and reorganize the drawers
- recognize the moments when you lack deliberation and mindfulness
- use less plastic
- work at the election polls
- prevent trouble before it arises
- when your energy is low, try doing breathing exercises or Sun Salutation
- buy two of every gift when holiday shopping and donate one

- light a candle when you practice yoga
- remove clutter from your workout space
- accept serendipity
- address the pain and conflict in your life
- curb your combative nature
- imagine a better life
- sit in a chair and trace your energy, feeling the vibration of your life-force energy from the top of your head, through your fingers, down your spine, through the soles of your feet
- let go of the desire to always be right
- bring your lunch to work in a reusable bag
- obey the Ten Commandments
- go into silence until the answer emerges
- cook dinner for someone
- record an oral history of the family
- repair a damaged family heirloom
- Real life starts with self-sacrifice (Thomas Carlyle)

- no matter where you are, you did not get there on your own
- donate all the clothes you no longer wear
- take your parents out to dinner
- take a break
- seek elegance rather than luxury
- feel mud between your toes
- be zealous
- don't try to control, subdue, or modify your thoughts
- put your conscious mind on a sabbatical
- sing in the shower
- visit the countries of your ancestors
- shed vanity
- pull up the anchor and let the boat drift
- be receptive to whatever unfolds
- let the business of the day fall into perspective
- break out of an old routine
- help each other grow

- all the happiness in the world comes from thinking of others; all the suffering in the world comes from thinking only of yourself
- develop 360-degree vision
- read Norman Vincent Peale's books
- find the yoga style that suits you
- if you are nervous, jumpy, overwrought, or otherwise on edge, take a moment to follow your breath
- what you see depends on how you see
- open your senses to the environment
- bring fresh flowers to work
- drink a glass of water while you are waiting for your coffee to perk
- turn telephone ringers off or down
- promote a society where no child is abused
- use a lake image in your meditation; the calm below the surface, any defilements or sediment sinking to the bottom

- if you do not use it, "lose" it
- before you get out of bed, think about why you are here
- take a pregnant woman out for a milkshake
- make a list of values you want to pass on to your children
- talk about happiness
- own your moments
- enjoy an Oreo cookie and milk
- take maps or an atlas when you go on a road trip
- take Communion
- avoid using products that harm any beings, either in their production or application
- follow the Buddha and follow your practice; learn the Four Noble Truths and enter the Noble Eightfold Path
- spend a day at an amusement park
- jump for joy on the inside
- take a child to your library's story hour

- find good friends
- give *The New York Times Book Review* to a friend who loves books but does not buy the paper
- share responsibility
- take turns changing diapers
- develop a household routine
- pick food in season whenever possible
- the more you let go, the lighter the mind becomes
- give your kids a say in how they use their discretionary time
- look at a problem as a test
- choose not to drink alcohol
- meditate for one minute of every hour throughout the day
- read about advances in science and technology
- watch someone's favorite TV program with him — even if you don't like it
- grow some of your own food

- rely less on recipes
- a positive attitude will affect the outcome positively
- offer a beverage to your plumber or electrician
- don't let someone's behavior determine your response
- let go of even the most subtle expectations
- give yourself a bouquet of flowers
- the perception of *chi* is the first step in learning to manage the energy that empowers you
- bring into your home only things you know to be interesting, educational, or entertaining
- detach from all things to become one with them
- refinish furniture yourself
- do things that create and reinforce happiness
- celebrate the first week of school
- enjoy the person you are right now
- for sloth and torpor, take a few deep breaths or go on a walk
- share what you love

- be an advocate for quality television programming
- live lightly on the land
- put increased care into the things you do and make
- periodically survey your life and see what areas need more attention
- frame and hang your marriage certificate
- before you do anything, ask yourself why you are doing it
- slow down your yoga practce
- write your living will
- don't try to solve all of your problems at once
- invite yourself to be happy in this moment
- applaud bright kids
- believe in the Golden Rule
- as much as you love someone, realize that you can't control that person's life
- write outdoors
- every problem comes from a selfish mind

- listen to your favorite music during stressful times
- partake of regional offerings on the menu
- sponsor someone for an Elderhostel
- master your past in the present or the past will master your future
- save someone from embarrassment by laughing with them
- ask a family member to pick a number from 1 to 10 and then deliver that many kisses
- live simply and with purity of heart
- listen to a friend's troubles
- make better food choices
- welcome inspiring messages
- get rid of outdated ideas
- support seasonal businesses
- dance whenever the spirit moves you
- spiritual maturity brings kindness to the heart
- learn to be happy in any surroundings

- for good luck and prosperity, place any of these on your desk: a cow, deer, dragon, tortoise, unicorn, fountain, crystal paperweight, or candy jar
- enjoy a cup of tea on the front steps in the sunshine
- give more than you're asked for
- stay close to teachers
- be able to laugh at yourself
- don't seek vengeance
- watch your blood pressure
- rejoice in your food
- take joy in the small things
- get to know the mind
- let life be more of a dance and less of a battle
- move in the direction your heart tells you to go
- hold your head high
- develop your spiritual muscles
- surprise someone with a homemade pie
- feed the soul

- think twice before burdening a friend with a secret
- watch the grass grow
- buy your children educational toys
- stay active through work, play, and community
- be honest, loving, and compassionate toward yourself
- remember the good within you
- the moment you pay attention to emotions,
  they lose their power over you
- go for a hike and enjoy the scenery
- get an hour's work done before anyone gets up
- empty the garbage pails in your home daily
- find joy in whatever needs to be done
- happiness cannot be found through great effort
  and willpower; it is already present
- give that which you most wish to receive
- be house-proud
- embrace the world as the gift it is: an apple is a gift,
  the color pink is a gift, the scent of a flower is a gift

- don't watch the news immediately before bedtime
- give away something you love to someone you love
- make a Saturday morning round of clean-the-house into something fun
- listen before you act
- nurture the unique talents of children
- express only those thoughts that will bring happiness to yourself and others
- encourage children to try new things
- identify the next step and take it
- be tactful
- choose your surroundings carefully
- say a morning prayer
- make a list of all the things you want to do with your life
- know what you can control and what you cannot
- everything counts, everyone counts
- allow feelings to come and go

- absorb the best of what each day has to offer
- it is not our preferences that cause problems, but our attachment to them
- live without need and without jealousy
- visit your neighbor
- make and keep a weekly date with your spouse
- don't cling to the hope that things will turn out a certain way
- listen to classical music during your lunch break
- Let food be your medicine and medicine be your food (Hippocrates)
- give from the heart
- do leg lifts to help alleviate lower back pain
- learn how to change your state of mind
- don't buy exercise equipment or hire a personal trainer — take a walk
- start to live the life you wish to live
- take time to laugh

instant karma

- take a casserole to the home of a couple with a newborn
- look into the intention of the source when deciding what to believe
- Kindness is more important than wisdom, and the recognition of this is the beginning of wisdom (Theodore I. Rubin)
- broaden your perspective
- resolve not to eat when standing or walking
- refrain from using speech that is hurtful
- discover what makes you feel most alive
- attend meetings at town hall
- cut out and share newspaper and magazine comics
- greet the mail deliverer
- see everything as though for the first time
- accept others as they are
- love the earth
- shop at going-out-of-business sales and auctions

- set television rules for your children
- One must be able to let things happen (Carl Jung)
- respect your body and mind
- exercise for an hour before breakfast
- recognition of the feeling of like and dislike — without reaction — cuts the karmic chain
- use baking soda as a nonabrasive cleaner for the home
- leave cheerful messages on others' voice mail
- think less about the people and things that bother you
- fulfill your potential as a person, spouse, and parent
- plan your work
- take the dog for a swim
- evaluate risks and benefits
- stop when you notice a pedestrian about to cross the road
- avoid eating food that is too hot or too cold
- be dogged and zealous about your practice
- treat yourself to a therapeutic massage

- plan next summer's family reunion
- plant a berry bush as a bird "feeder"
- delight someone
- become what you are capable of becoming
- define progress as taking two small steps forward for each step back
- stay useful, whatever your age
- hold nothing back from life
- volunteer to work the concession stand for the school
- keep yourself from getting too hungry, too angry, too lonely, or too tired
- do one thing really well
- join a friendly gym
- make sure your facts are correct
- take advantage of "found time"
- say yes when you really mean it
- write a note that says "need you"
- good posture can improve your well-being

- work as a tutor
- seek to transform enemies into allies
- pay attention to details
- try using the mantra from the *Prajnaparamita Sutra*: *gatte gatte parasamgatte bodhi svaha*
- if you can inhale and hold seven breaths, your oxygen will be completely circulated through your blood system, and you shall not need whatever you were craving/longing to have
- live with wonder
- say the sentimental grateful things that we all feel but are often too scared to speak aloud
- lovingly care for the place where you live
- be kinder, more gentle, more forgiving of the people around you
- indulge in reflection and reasoning
- welcome the new kid at school
- refuse to put a label on everything you do

- practice doing nothing
- leave a light on for someone who is out at night
- collect kindling with a child on a crisp autumn afternoon
- use a good mind well
- know pleasant ways to keep yourself company
- invite a neighbor over for an impromptu dinner
- present your child with opportunities to be self-reliant
- challenge your basic mind-set
- have mental rehearsals for steps toward your goal
- find the time
- do something good
- out-tension tension by tightening your muscles and releasing
- be content with life as it is
- remember the virtues of others
- sing along with your favorite singer
- learn how to pack a suitcase efficiently

- savor the time you spend with the people who matter
- enjoy goofing off
- take joy in serving others
- abolish yelling
- show love to your fellow human beings and you are showing love to your God
- choose to look forward to something when you get up in the morning
- house-sit for a neighbor
- go beyond ordinary thought
- make favorite foods for a family picnic
- great wake-up scents are tangerine, orange, bergamot, rosemary, eucalyptus, lemon, lime, jasmine, rose, pine, and lavender
- cleanse your mind of flaws little by little
- support a safe cure for obesity
- speak gently
- let others aspire to what might benefit them most

- stir up warm, friendly feelings on a cold morning
- be easily pleased
- do for others what you want them to do for you
- give complimentary nicknames
- keep your expectations realistic
- practice *shavasana* (Corpse Pose) to give your mind a mini-vacation
- you already possess all the material from which to create your ideal self
- change painful situations
- stand like a mountain
- To eat is human, to digest divine (Charles T. Copeland)
- accept your own limitations
- hold tight to your ideals
- discover that good is good enough
- direct your energies positively
- establish priority goals — both short- and long-term — for your life

- know what to overlook
- don't be encumbered by unnecessary possessions
- find good in everything
- care about spelling
- practice must flow like a river — quietly, smoothly, continuously
- when you have nothing to say, say nothing
- eat at a moderate pace
- talk gently
- listen to your heart of hearts
- give yourself a kick in the seat of your pants
- pick your own fruits and vegetables at an organic farm
- at dinnertime, think of three to four things for which you are thankful
- perform one household chore slowly and patiently
- leave the talking to others
- donate an ant farm to a kindergarten
- let go of fear

185 instant karma

- give an enormous striped lollipop to a child
- learn what is necessary and what is not
- set your sights high
- leave magazines at work for others to enjoy
- choose to drink water
- happiness comes not from reaching out but from letting go
- regard nothing as your own
- perform small acts of grace
- choose well-crafted products
- have a pleasant chat with your neighbor
- make use of all your resources
- say "I love you" first — and often
- do just one thing at a time
- give yourself all the credit you are due
- shed your past like a snake's skin
- forgive real and imaginary injustices
- don't criticize

- find yourself in someone else
- learn to use exercise as a way to develop higher levels of awareness
- read the wisdom of Winnie the Pooh to children
- see with your heart
- know where your children are
- do the Soto Zen face-the-wall meditation, sitting 12 to 18 inches from a completely blank wall
- spend fifteen minutes each day doing something you really enjoy
- cuddle up with the kids and a good book
- respect the natural cycles of life
- stand straight, your head held as if suspended by a thread from the sky
- write to an activist whom you admire
- give yourself pep talks
- eat simply
- always keep something in reserve

- work with a mindfulness discipline to protect your physical and mental well-being
- discover the present
- be passionate about something you can count on to be there — not another person, but an interest
- visit someone you have not seen in a very long time
- enjoy the pleasure of discovery
- relax, enjoy, laugh, play
- help someone find a lost pet
- see the humor in life every day
- put your house in order
- speak only when your words are better than your silence
- develop avocations
- look at everything and everybody as though you're seeing them for the first time
- read one of Alan Watts's books on Zen
- allow your flower garden to be picked

- stay on the path
- rejuvenate tired eyes by focusing on something near and then far
- treat the cause, not the symptom
- make someone laugh
- help someone who needs it
- become aware of how your body moves
- be your own light and your own refuge
- donate to Habitat for Humanity
- banish negative thoughts about yourself
- heal a wound
- spend 20 to 30 minutes a day preparing food
- make the person you are with feel comfortable
- happiness is being free from desires
- do your spiritual exercises over and over again
- release your tension as you focus your breathing
- try to cultivate a nonjudgmental awareness, a "just knowing"

- indulge yourself often in what you do well
- deliver hope
- say a prayer prior to ending a meditation session
- slow down your internal clock
- be warm and affectionate according to others' needs
- speak about your home in a positive way
- live as well as possible
- use a "speed cleaning" method for your house
- give yourself first what you seek from others
- happiness is not dependent on how much you have
- quiet your mind and transcend your ego
- Those who bring sunshine to the lives of others cannot keep it from themselves (James M. Barrie)
- say good-bye to a bad mood
- know when to lead and when to follow
- know what to do in a power failure
- drink peppermint tea to soothe your stomach
- stop buying things you don't need

- watch public TV
- join the library's summer book club
- make a contribution
- show children that happiness is not created through indulgence
- use forward-bending yoga postures to help you internalize and quiet your mind
- appreciate street musicians
- keep lists of words to look up in dictionaries
- make a list of ten books you would like to read purely for pleasure
- do a stream-of-consciousness exercise
- practice visualization at night as you fade off to sleep
- arrange for a family conference call on a special day
- Every minute you are angry, you lose sixty seconds of happiness (Ralph Waldo Emerson)
- develop an awareness of what is actually going on in your body

- eat foods that agree with your constitution
- dare to make mistakes
- sitting cross-legged, do twenty-six spinal twists for the liver and spleen, with hands on shoulders and elbows up
- be really good at something
- keep learning
- do not attempt to be a particular type of person
- compliment your mate in front of your children, parents, and friends
- take responsibility for what you say
- remember that what is known directly is absolutely yours
- do your work, then step back
- donate unused tyke bikes
- create a room that is truly restful
- exercise your tension away
- get to know your employees, students, or players

instant karma

- associate with like-minded people
- put a sunbonnet on a baby
- if you have too much to do, take a nap
- create easy-to-follow house rules
- make sundaes for kids who help you on errands
- when a child speaks, really listen
- conquer fear by doing the things you fear to do
- spray cologne in stinky sneakers
- after you read the newspaper, leave it neat and in order
- anonymously mail money to someone who needs it
- smile at people — it will unclench your teeth and relax your face
- nurture creativity
- walk in silence, promote the integration of muscles, mind, and spirit
- share your dessert
- do the worst task first

- eat foods that rekindle good childhood memories
- take advantage of an advantage
- surround yourself with things that make you feel happy
- inscribe a book you give to someone
- serve as an altar person
- point all of your goals in the same direction
- bring home a favorite magazine for someone
- take mindful time-outs
- teach your children to love orderliness
- spend a day hibernating
- be an engaging storyteller
- don't disappoint those who depend on you
- bestow a favor, then forget it
- contemplate the universe
- leave a love or friendship note on a car
- be friendly, gracious, and flexible
- say, "I can do this"

- be a friend who can always be counted on
- admit with good cheer that someone else was right
- when you feel great, let your face show it
- know how to wait
- pursue old-fashioned hobbies, games, and activities
- create a personal vision
- don't fight back
- read *The Dhammapada*
- bring touches of nature indoors
- baby-sit the grandchildren
- have a party for no special reason
- cry when you feel like it
- let others take responsibility for their own lives
- Be attentive to what you do; never consider anything unworthy of your attention (Confucius)
- establish healthy living habits
- accept your mistakes
- engage in thoughtful solitude

- have a beginner's mind: be willing to see everything as if for the first time
- support an animal advocacy group
- to be happy, decide to stop being unhappy
- blow your own horn
- let go of your judgmental self-consciousness
- give a cornflower bouquet to a sick friend
- make sure the birthday person feels truly celebrated
- convert your home to solar energy
- make eye contact, even with strangers
- let your children overhear you complimenting them to other adults
- be conscientious
- videotape, photograph, or record events
- chop your own wood
- share your professional know-how
- tend to the little rips, tears, and loose buttons of life
- invent new ways of thinking about the same old things

- indulge in long baths
- surprise your mom with fresh flowers
- give someone a cozy robe in the morning
- karma has no deadline
- clean your house with pure water, lemon, and vinegar with clear scents — eucalyptus, sage, lavender, pine
- teach Sunday school
- repetitions of mantras (*japa*) may be counted using a string of 108 mala beads (hold in right hand, count using thumb and middle finger)
- try to be aware of what others are thinking and feeling
- reassess your coping strategies for managing stress
- listen to your favorite music
- live your life on nature's time schedule
- use libraries and reference books
- buy only high-quality oil, vinegar, and salt
- treat yourself as you would a dear friend
- read books that lift your spirit

- be happy without having a reason
- try to eat one meal a day in silence
- Happiness depends upon ourselves (Aristotle)
- lean forward as you listen to others
- donate an art box to a needy child
- learn to say no
- call to let someone know you're thinking of them
- ask: is this item useful to me? do I love it? if not, why do I want to keep it?
- love the questions
- do the qigong "Scoop the Stream" exercise
- sit in a child's swing
- the ultimate goal of the yogi is to help you achieve your own experience of truth
- get good grades
- set your sights higher
- end speed-reading, quick-fixing, rush-houring, fast-tracking, hustling and bustling

- invite adventure
- easy does it
- don't put things off; tie up loose ends as you go
- try to practice a disinterested acceptance
- wear clothes someone gave you when you see them
- separate the recycling for the garbage pickup
- have a heart-to-heart with Dad
- develop your willpower bit by bit
- taste food to satiate your mind
- think and speak well of your health
- live beneath your means
- lend a favorite book
- be at home wherever you find yourself
- learn the words to the national anthem
- revisit Henry David Thoreau's *Walden* to learn about his philosophy of simple living
- develop concentration so completely that nothing but an emergency can distract you

- organize a child's favorite collection
- when we have no expectations, there are no disappointments
- thank the security guards where you work
- sample Kikan koans, which lead to a better understanding of the differentiated world as seen through the eye of enlightenment
- avoid pettiness and triviality
- find ways to serve the world
- experiment with morning foods until you find what sustains you until lunchtime
- sing "You'll Never Walk Alone" whenever you need to
- organize cleaning parties
- do the Breath of Fire: a rapid inhalation and exhalation through your nose that strengthens your nervous system and energizes you
- feel your anger thoroughly but don't get stuck
- ignore pressure to win

- expand your intellectual perspective
- listen to old people
- throw a surprise party for someone
- have the courage to pursue new ideas
- try to make at least one person feel better each day because of something you say
- volunteer to be a big brother or sister
- reflecting on the law of karma brings an appreciation of one's life
- carpool
- be thankful under all circumstances
- give an engagement gift
- yoga tones the inner body as well as the outer body
- try to practice yoga six days out of seven
- use herbs and spices as natural air fresheners
- keep growing
- play gentle music, soften the lighting, let fresh air in, light a candle

- if something bad happens, try to get over it quickly
- emulate role models
- have consideration for others
- allow others to make mistakes
- seek truth in the depths of your own heart
- to meditate, sit comfortably with your back straight, head erect, and chin tucked in slightly
- organize your errands before you leave the house
- eat a fruit or vegetable you've never tried before
- do the Eagle Pose to improve balance and concentration, develop the ankles, remove shoulder stiffness
- focus on a meditation object
- solicit feedback from friends, relations, and colleagues
- practice directing healing energy
- wisdom is revealed through action, not talk
- To be wronged is nothing unless you continue to remember it (Confucius)

- tell someone she's beautiful
- choose your respones
- make people feel important
- make your love for truth greater than your need to be right
- use scents to create an atmosphere of calm and tranquility
- improve the atmosphere in which you live
- donate groceries to a local food bank
- discover the Zen koan Joshu's Mu
- help old friends grow old
- nurture awareness in every moment of your life
- go on a silent hike
- rid yourself of the impression that you are indispensable
- spend a "vacation" in silent retreat
- meditation has little to do with time and much to do with your effort

- give gifts spontaneously
- learn to defuse your energy through relaxation
- finish unfinished business
- wish for the happiness of others
- practice mindful walking and deep listening all day long, examples of the Four Noble Truths in action
- be concise
- concentrate on what is really important to you
- emphasize personal accountability
- commit to a project
- encourage bilingualism
- people become what they expect themselves to become
- establish a meditation group
- reserve a seat for a friend
- focus your effort on the present
- teach others how to treat you by the way you treat yourself

- use twenty minutes to think or relax
- don't interrupt someone when they are watching their favorite TV show
- why be happy with more if you can be happy with less?
- burn a pink candle to increase loving feelings and enhance friendship
- take a walk in the park on the first warm day of spring
- feel satisfied with the rightness of the world
- wash the dishes when it's not your turn
- respect someone by learning from them
- sweat-inducing exercise helps control the appetite
- get something fixed that has been broken
- go sledding
- don't purchase items that belonged to someone who died, was divorced, went bankrupt, or was fired
- cool off before responding to provocation
- Half a loaf is better than none (Anonymous)
- enlarge your world

- throw a party for an older person celebrating a significant birthday
- let someone win at tic-tac-toe
- appreciate the little things in life
- walk the dog for someone who is laid up
- excellence resides in quality and not in quantity
- meditate
- remove all anxious fears concerning the future
- The greatest truths are the simplest, and so are the greatest men (Augustus J.C. Hare)
- work without complaining
- to be frugal means to have a high joy-to-stuff ratio
- nothing is permanent except impermanence
- use your oven efficiently
- take a mini-break
- avoid drinking excessive amounts of any one kind of tea
- open yourself to your intuition

- budget time as if it were money
- envelop yourself with calm
- leave candies on the chairs of coworkers
- remove television and radio from the dining and cooking areas
- when you make a mistake, admit it, correct it, and move on
- everything you do and how you do it matters
- establish and maintain a healthy authority over your children
- love someone for who and what they are, without conditions
- study history
- make the best possible choice
- ignore fads
- learn a relaxation routine
- create order in your house and office
- encourage others to succeed beyond their abilities

- be the master of yourself in every situation
- train yourself to become more yielding, balanced, and flexible
- speak your truth without trying to control others
- change behaviors that do not have positive effects
- use the "railway tunnel" meditation to leave troubles behind, gain perspective, and focus on the here and now
- take care of your tools
- review the entire day as if you were watching a video
- clean the house as a family
- ask, listen, and hear to determine the wants and needs of others
- send travel postcards to friends
- be a teacher's assistant
- go for a morning swim
- toast and butter a pastry for a loved one
- consider and reflect

- live everything!
- wear down your restlessness
- play first and work later
- visit the bookmobile
- toil until some good is accomplished
- make a list of everything you want to accomplish by the end of the year
- learn to function on less sleep when you need to
- when you hear a kind word spoken about a friend, tell them so
- let positive energy flow through you
- take up leisure activities that please and satisfy you
- aim for others' abilities to surpass your own
- include your kids while cooking
- imagine how someone might be feeling and what they would like to hear
- patronize rural roadside stands
- be long on patience

- experience a journey of endless surprises
- aim to be happy day by day
- hire someone to serenade your loved one with "your song"
- curling up with a cat or walking the dog can create a naturally meditative state
- remove a roadblock
- learn to live by learning to let go
- teach a kid to ride a bike
- expand on different possibilities
- surprise and delight children
- support your child as he or she learns
- how much will fulfilling a particular desire mean at the end of life?
- speak calmly instead of yelling
- mail a card to your child, even if you haven't gone away
- act wisely in the face of difficult situations

- create a mural on paper with kids
- eat a Puritan dinner: salad, fruit, cereal and milk, or baked potato
- get a real life
- raise your ecological consciousness
- take children to fireworks displays
- set a date to break a bad habit and stick to it
- walk your anger away
- don't criticize family or friends
- carry money without spending it
- love the most difficult part of yourself
- be strengthened by hardship
- examine both short-range and the long-range
- give someone a snuggly gift, like a hot water bottle or something cashmere
- Never put off till tomorrow what you can do today (Lord Chesterfield)
- shower with your eyes closed

- practice *uddiyana*: after exhaling completely, pull the abdomen up and back toward the spine
- contract the muscles of your pelvic area and navel to do a "root lock" — a small internal exercise
- prevent fires
- give solace to others
- concentrate on filling each day with moments that gratify you
- safeguard your mind and reason
- let go when you really want to hold on
- start a stock portfolio or IRA in your child's name
- try yoga to ease the pain of carpal tunnel syndrome
- appreciate yourself
- be more acutely aware of shapes and textures, sounds, colors, and scents
- share leftovers
- make scones and tea for your sister
- ask a person to tell you a story of his or her youth

- in a cross-legged position, do a spinal flex forward (chest up) and backward (rolling back), which stimulates the first chakra
- build something from what stands in your way
- balancing yin and yang brings peace of mind
- provide your mate with a get-away-from-it-all time
- life is neither a race nor a competition
- share a sunset with someone
- plan ways to combine two or three similar tasks
- do the right thing at the right time
- buy a bunch of daffodils on your way home
- never stop wooing your beloved
- do something each day just for you
- talk to children at their eye level
- breathe all the way in and all the way out
- practice Camel Pose, a kneeling backbend
- treasure-hunt with a favorite youngster
- scan newspapers and magazines

 instant karma

- remember that a word is an action
- blow kisses across the room
- That load becomes light which is cheerfully borne (Ovid)
- respect the wishes of others when they say no
- take responsibility for all your actions
- become aware of the demands you place on yourself and others
- pay attention in day-to-day life
- prioritize what really matters
- wake someone with the aroma of hot coffee
- listen to a book-on-tape on your way to work
- Nothing can bring you peace but yourself (Ralph Waldo Emerson)
- don't be too serious
- encourage kids to submit articles and drawings to the kids' page in the newspaper
- take delight in the welfare and happiness of others

- read a time management book and put the suggestions into practice
- turn off political commercials
- overtip
- slow down long enough to examine your habits
- let go of wasteful speech and idle gossip
- come up against big challenges
- relax in a steam room
- learn how to change a tire
- as dharma fills us, it changes our outlook and eventually brings us to right view
- find the Big Dipper and other constellations
- save the classifieds for a job hunter
- be appreciative
- keep a record of the lessons you've learned
- bring a treat home for someone who could not join you for dinner
- be present and aware

- never miss a chance to send flowers
- drive with patience
- affirm the positive in others
- live your life in happiness, even when those around you lead lives that are unhealthy
- run a marathon
- work with care and attention
- impose deadlines for every project you do
- define a successful day by how much attention you pay to your inner life
- display your wedding gifts
- stand at the edge of a frontier (artistic, literary, scientific)
- think of being in a crowd as being part of a zoo
- go to funny movies
- take your time
- don't worry about what you didn't accomplish yesterday

- give away what you want most (love, money, gratitude)
- when you see someone you love, say, "*namaste,*" which means "I behold the divine in you."
- hide all the clocks in your house for one day
- cultivate an open mind
- go with your initial, intuitive response
- love the world as yourself
- eat lower on the food chain
- happy cooks make happy food
- donate new stuffed animals and toys to a shelter
- when cabin fever sets in, go somewhere for a change of scene
- build your morality
- surprise a child with an inexpensive toy
- vote for a reasonable increase in the school budget
- redraw your view of the world with visualization
- do not follow the crowd, but don't complain about those who do

- line closet shelves with scented paper
- don't get upset, anxious, or angry about things over which you have no power
- pop popcorn in the fireplace
- peruse the sale racks
- clean off your desk
- make up an album of your child's memorabilia
- do what you say and say what you mean
- do squats (also called Crow Pose), extending your arms in front, hands clasped; hold for one to three minutes
- the minute you don't want power, you will have more than you ever dreamed possible
- overcome every insecurity
- tell the truth and expect the truth
- eliminate racial prejudice
- Knowledge will not always take the place of simple observation (Arnold Lobel)

- observe the effect that foods have on your body
- keep a journal to record your insights and questions
- use externalization to liberate yourself from pain
- shop early for the holidays
- help save the nation's wetlands
- take a multivitamin
- sweep chimneys, take up carpets, paint the kitchen
- write your resolutions down
- buy healthy food, not diet food
- know when to work and when to play
- try to put yourself in situations where there is an abundance of good choices
- act with consideration
- do not be afraid to get older
- snack on dried fruit
- wake up in the morning with a pleasant thought
- it's not that nothing matters, but that everything matters equally

- send care packages of food to kids at camp or college
- buy someone a pair of slippers
- play classical music while cleaning or cooking
- support politicians who work for prenatal care for all
- express thanks often
- help improve the local public library
- keep your lawn neat and litter-free
- select a livelihood that reflects your ethics
- stretch your back on a daily basis
- get closer to your Higher Power
- take a family bike ride
- resolve not to magnify small problems
- hang on to your dreams
- practice nonattachment
- when you buy a new coat, take a used one to the homeless shelter
- support public television
- always keep your priorities in perspective

- contemplate the virtues of the Buddha
- every day is a good day
- become familiar with the workings of your state and local government
- know when and how to be satisfied
- take time every day to sit quietly and listen
- eat somewhere new: outside, on the porch, on the floor
- nothing much happens unless you believe in it
- do not give way to every common impulse
- appreciate turbulence
- learn some basic cooking to help yourself maintain a healthy weight
- endow a scholarship
- always try to be open with others so that they will be open with you
- walk softly, live gently
- stop, sit down, and become aware of your breathing several times throughout the day

 instant karma

- expand
- release tension with gentle head and shoulder rolls
- be worthy
- everybody starts with 168 hours a week
- eat at least one raw salad every day
- learn more about the English language
- eat fruit, bagels, or English muffins instead of doughnuts and pastries
- never run out of things to do
- think about abundance instead of lack
- whenever you are true to yourself, you will be true to others
- look for the best in new ideas
- revel in age, do not regret it
- think healthy, positive, noble thoughts
- be courageous enough to express a unique vision
- don't make people wait for an important answer
- **plant a community garden**

- do what you think is necessary
- patronize the little store on the corner
- try a new variety of tea
- practice the art of relaxation
- buy movie tickets for the person standing in line behind you
- take part in trust-building activities
- To live means to be aware, joyously, drunkenly, serenely, divinely aware (Henry Miller)
- give back to your K–12 schools
- remember that your life matters more than your size
- try to make friends everywhere you go
- receive a guest warmly
- play bingo at a senior center
- write a poem as part of a wedding gift
- avoid eating on the run
- wear a warm afghan instead of turning up the heat
- appreciate the value of time

- eat just a little less
- forgive your parents
- give back rubs without being asked
- add to someone's collection
- make a confession while you still have the chance
- encourage restaurants to donate leftovers to the hungry
- stay centered or return to your center
- when angry, talk to yourself the same way you would talk to an upset friend
- express gratitude fully and freely
- develop savoir faire
- don't look ahead
- grow watermelons and pumpkins
- respect others' traditions
- don't use videos, television, or the computer as a baby-sitter for your kids
- don't become your state of mind

- consider the long-term effects of your words and actions
- be kind to all living beings
- take your time and don't say things impulsively
- throw a holiday party
- refuse to be negative
- make some of your own clothes
- let all things take their course
- love what you do for a living or change what you do
- enjoy a little wine with dinner
- see others' suffering as your own
- be aware of the five hindrances: desire, aversion, sleepiness, restlessness, doubt
- wait out a craving for at least ten minutes
- see the infinite, the universal
- always rely on inner resources
- know what your life's purpose is
- don't mistake your thoughts for who you are

- remember that principles are better than rules
- if we train our breathing, we can control our emotions
- hang out happily
- paint your rooms a color you look and feel good in
- learn first aid
- hire a caterer to fix a romantic dinner for you and your mate
- instead of asking what's wrong, ask what's not wrong?
- if you have a sugar addiction, avoid sugar altogether
- be soft-spoken
- consciously enjoy the process of changing
- follow the path of least resistance
- applaud loudly
- use a tongue scraper to remove toxins that accumulate during the night
- enhance your environment
- eat soup more often
- eat when you are relaxed

- look for the extraordinary in the ordinary
- let certain problems resolve themselves naturally
- clear your head
- take time to play
- store notes and memorabilia in a family "time capsule"
- take stock of your current condition and see how you can balance it
- look at textbooks as cumulative knowledge
- maintain apple-pie order
- in every moment you have a choice
- send a baseball fan to see spring training
- link yourself with a great cause
- give a dozen hugs a day
- it is our intentions that create karma
- offer equal pay for equal work
- give away attic junk to people who can use it
- open yourself to the Tao, then trust your natural responses and everything will fall into place

- acknowledge joys and vicissitudes
- do the *chi* ball exercise: stand squarely but relaxed with hands at waist level; practice imagining that you are holding a ball of energy
- relinquish craving, clinging, and attachment to allow nirvana to seep in
- give someone a something-of-the-month subscription
- balance your checkbook
- listen to your kids
- brainstorm
- let go/forgive/accept
- experiment
- offer to push a child on a swing
- make plans you can look forward to
- delight kids with clever stocking stuffers
- whenever you see an opportunity to do something that brings peace or kindness into the world, do it!
- watch and listen for children's needs

- challenge your trunk/torso with Pilates leg circles
- keep birthdays simple
- honor your own best impulses
- live in detail
- stop giving energy to the things you don't believe in
- learn to focus
- Always dream and shoot higher than you know you can do (William Faulkner)
- create a committed relationship and keep it exciting
- accept things as they are
- make home-brewed window cleaner of vinegar and water with a drop of liquid soap
- add fresh spinach to salads and sandwiches
- engage in positive business practices
- hold an umbrella over someone if it's raining
- watch your thoughts; they become words
- use your time wisely
- keep a pen and paper handy

 instant karma

- don't cling too tightly to anything
- don't mistake pleasure for happiness
- shop at organic food markets
- offer comfort
- relax about money
- play with enthusiasm
- read directions carefully
- take each step as it comes
- be ecologically aware
- never spend your money before you have it
- believe that every problem has a solution
- whatever you wish for, drop it deliberately, knowing that you don't really need it
- nothing can erase your good deeds
- share/give/receive
- save rainwater for watering your plants
- if you wish to see the truth, hold no opinions for or against anything

- return phone calls promptly
- donate a little money, time, or both on a regular basis
- pay off your loans
- start the day by reaffirming your intention always to speak with compassion and love
- do not start anything for profit that would cause harm
- live right instead of trying to prove you are right
- listen to the president's speeches
- jump at the opportunity for children to travel
- have respect for detail
- strength is knowing how to yield
- make a huge valentine cookie for your child
- have strategies for coping with stressful situations
- act as though it were impossible to fail
- give up your four o'clock candy bar
- associate with people who are on the same path
- show another camper how to braid gimp
- soothe yourself to sleep with comforting rituals

- don't laugh at new ideas
- when you eat well, your reward is feeling better
- visit with people from different cultures
- turn off the television for today
- stop — and be present
- tell a friend, "You did great!"
- visit a Shaker community
- make snacks for the Monday night football gang
- Buddhism's Noble Silence is practiced with no radio, no phone, no television, no writing, no reading, no Internet
- send aid to the victims of an international disaster
- return your shopping cart to its place
- explore what it means to create a sacred space
- start over if necessary
- help someone figure out a solution instead of giving advice
- Follow your bliss (Joseph Campbell)

- let your feelings flow through you, then let them end
- don't use up your energy feeling angry and overwhelmed
- see the beauty in every religious ceremony
- give something away today
- keep at it after others have given up
- eliminate any negative tone from your speech
- try vegetarianism a day at a time and note how you feel
- regard everything you do as a learning experience
- plant tulips at Thanksgiving
- work toward the abolishment of slavery in the world
- burn a brown candle to protect pets and solve home problems
- practice restraint with small desires to give yourself strength of mind when there are powerful desires
- listen to your feelings
- read how-to books
- draw and doodle

 instant karma

- do yoga in your office chair, at your desk
- feed birds in the winter
- walk with integrity
- buy or make a holiday decoration for someone
- capture the anticipation felt by a child awaking on Christmas morning
- sew or write during a child's nap
- think of what you have instead of what you want
- study other cultures' ideas of simple living
- consider all things to be an illusion
- whenever you get up from sitting, take one breath and shift your attention to your feet
- celebrate each of the seasons
- acquire a virtue today
- practice loving feelings toward everyone you meet
- have a baby's sneakers bronzed
- adopt a positive attitude in the face of difficulty
- buy soft furniture

- use conflict to inspire creativity
- remember good times together
- put Grandpa's best stories on tape
- After examining and analyzing a teaching, if you find it to be kind, conducive to the good and the benefit and welfare of others, believe and cling to it (Buddha)
- give praise and respect
- listen to that hunch
- look for quality workmanship
- smile just for the fun of it
- persevere in the face of obstacles
- fill your house with equal parts of love, hope, and peace
- help a kid who squirms in church
- think of the day ahead as an adventure
- don't use Styrofoam
- do what is right even when everyone else doesn't

- refrain from all intoxicants and addictive substances for one month
- love yourself just the way you are
- have a nurturing side
- help someone
- believe that government is the servant of the people
- use kind words to defuse someone else's unhappiness
- serenade someone
- improve your handwriting
- as a parent, set limits
- warm a towel for someone who is taking a shower
- learn to enjoy the fresh taste of less-processed foods
- teach a child the alphabet
- play your part in life, but never forget that it is only a role
- ask yourself: does drinking alcohol support my efforts to live with less delusion? does it sabotage my moment-to-moment awareness?

- give a foot massage
- start slow, stay steady
- "soften" your eyes by relaxing the muscles of your forehead, face, and jaw
- take kids on a wheelbarrow ride
- do less talking
- outwit denial by verbalizing the truth
- shop locally whenever possible
- if you seek wisdom over opportunity, opportunity will usually follow
- watch *The Dead Poets Society*
- make a brown-bag lunch for someone
- use alternative transportation like walking and biking
- "adopt" a nursing home resident and visit him or her regularly
- give great hugs
- take an interest in the lives of others
- give a train set to a children's hospital

- parents who consume mindfully will teach their children to exercise similar self-control
- be brave enough to be ordinary
- find your voice to ask for what you want
- calm your body as you breathe in; smile as you breathe out
- resolve never to go to bed angry
- mindfulness is making responsibilities a labor of love
- accumulate merit
- cultivate an expanded, open mind
- do one thing at a time
- spend Saturday at a state park or in a museum
- do preventive maintenance
- flaunt your flaws
- keep the speed limit
- take a deep breath and feel the diaphragm muscle move downward on inhalation and upward on exhalation

- give each person you love the thing they want most
- learn to meditate for relaxation
- accept yourself and the whole world will accept you
- let go of whatever holds you back
- burn a white candle to promote peace and spirituality
- eat a wide variety of fruits
- help out with a church event
- in the morning, eat a great deal of fruit and drink a lot of fluids
- when we accept situations for what they are, we become more effective in influencing them
- practice letting go one layer at a time
- You can't change the body without changing the mind, and you can't change the mind without changing the body (Moshe Feldenkrais)
- let go of foolish pride
- love your gray hairs
- try holotropic breathwork

- eat out once a week
- spend time with those you care about
- send a free pizza to a friend or neighbor
- learn to love and honor your body
- go on a Saturday picnic instead of shopping at a mall
- fly kites with kids
- open a book to any page and let that paragraph or line inspire you
- bake your own bread
- reward yourself with a small gift whenever you complete an unpleasant task
- go with the current and let it lift you free
- practice the mantra *there is always enough*
- with a lot of giving and a little taking you will get what you need
- bring in the daily mail for elderly neighbors
- enroll yourself and your dog in obedience school
- there is no need to attain anything

- learn to recognize what will or will not bring harmony to your life
- whenever your mind wanders, simply begin again
- be courageous
- when the sun rises, think of your life as just beginning
- be a lamp, or a lifeboat, or a ladder
- use the good silver
- love someone
- begin the process of "mental noting" in your daily life
- know how to take and give hints
- practice the Tree Pose to improve balance, concentration, and mindfulness
- cheer someone on
- find a "life song," a mantralike string of three or four syllables arranged in a pattern unique to you
- associate with optimists
- donate to churches, synagogues, mosques, monasteries, and nunneries

- become the most positive person you know
- follow the yoga niyamas: be pure, be content,
  be disciplined, be studious, be devoted
- say little
- drop off an apple pie at the police department
- just have coffee on a coffee break — don't try to do
  something else at the same time
- give a mantra your whole attention
- love those whom no one else loves
- place a quarter in a gumball machine
- respect the customs of other cultures
- give willfulness a rest
- ignore the sayings and doings of others
- there is nothing to like or dislike
- use half of what you use now
- say nice things to people
- eat from the four basic food groups
- make the best of what you have

- get down on the floor once a day and stretch mindfully, staying in touch with your breathing
- take up painting
- do yoga headstands
- develop interest in life as you see it, in people, things, literature, music
- prefer enduring satisfaction to immediate gratification
- repair broken things
- eat a light supper
- take the bounties given to you and don't ask for more
- make a Zen painting, expressing the "oatness" of an oat or the "treeness" of a tree
- find what you really care about and use that as the basis of your spiritual practice
- be patient in the checkout line
- leave time for small, sacred rituals in your life
- if you've lost your sense of humor — find it as soon as possible!

- your expression is the most important thing you wear
- contribute to a newspaper that focuses on good news
- don't try to change others
- avoid mindless attention to presumed duty
- imagine that you are in a protective bubble that reflects negative feelings back to those who give them off
- bring chilled orange or tomato juice to someone who is sick
- rejoice in time alone
- take healthy food to eat at the movies
- immerse yourself in the process
- send flowers to your dearest friend for no reason
- give an elderly person a pampering gift — massage, manicure, facial, hair appointment
- You are the architect of your life and you decide your destiny (Swami Rama)
- spend some time listening to yourself
- forgive those who have hurt you

- slow down enough to walk beside people
- for one week, act on every single thought of generosity that arises spontaneously in your heart
- allow people to be as they are, rather than having fixed ideas of what you want them to be
- grow and understand one another
- step delicately
- give anonymously to charity
- empty your mind of emotions that serve no purpose
- break a difficult mission into steps
- live your yoga
- name your house
- position your head over your spine and you will relieve a constant source of muscle tension
- put off procrastination
- ask, what did I once love to do that I am not doing now? and take it up again
- eliminate waste in cooking

 instant karma

- keep your commitments even when it hurts
- become a volunteer reading tutor
- commit yourself to growth
- do what makes your juices flow
- get up and start work before your boss
- hunt down good buys
- give yourself freedom to fail
- trust what is offered
- wave to neighbors as you ride by
- shower with products made with essential oils
- exchange enlightening interests
- join hands with those you love
- boost your mood with chocolate
- let yourself fall madly in love
- practice walking in a circle to reach the Tao
- be creative with the time you have
- bathe mindfully
- ignore your negative thoughts

- get rid of things you've been keeping "just in case"
- keep personal and financial records in order
- give someone a basket filled with miniature boxes of guest soaps, shampoos, perfumes
- invite a friend to attend a class with you
- breathe deeply
- when you have inner peace, you are less distracted by your wants, needs, desires, and concerns
- after the kids go to bed, savor the silence of the night
- spray your sheets with favorite bedtime scents
- before starting the car, know where you are going
- sit in a kneeling position, place both palms on the floor and bow to touch your third eye point (the sixth chakra) to the floor to alleviate depression and enhance intuition
- invite a family member somewhere they've never been
- make your mark on the world
- praise the cook

- look at what solutions are right in front of you
- support mom-and-pop businesses
- create a climate of hope
- satisfy your sweet tooth with fruit
- learn Space Clearing (feng shui)
- teach someone something they did not know
- tell someone, "No problem!" and mean it
- listen to a comedy recording
- leave nature undisturbed
- develop a silent practice
- ease chronic pain with hypnosis and relaxation techniques like yoga
- find ways to cut down on driving time
- ignore the trivial
- help others learn how to take care of themselves
- take refresher courses
- eat a big salad before you go to a restaurant
- cultivate flexible thinking

- stay calm in busy times
- be especially courteous and patient with older people
- invite someone over for iced tea
- reawaken your curiosity about nature
- the more single-mindedly you pursue material and sensual satisfaction, the more it will seem to elude you
- listen without judgment and with an open mind
- work to save an endangered animal
- be a beginner
- develop a realistic view of your body
- eat plenty of protein
- pack cookies in popped corn and send them to a sibling
- your sense of self and peace of mind should originate within
- share your ice cream
- the early bird catches the worm
- offer thanks for the beauty and goodness in the world

- let friends help
- go away for a weekend in the country
- take time every day for meditation
- learn to work with, not fight, pressure
- nix nighttime noshing
- show your love for your mate even when you do not feel like it
- give your hairstylist or barber a Christmas gift
- transforming the mind is a slow and gradual process
- give your mom a certificate to a day spa
- never seek vengeance
- be big enough to do a little task
- serve up casual Friday dinners
- know all the relevant facts
- give rest to your tongue more often than to your hands
- set reasonable bedtimes for yourself and kids
- open yourself to feelings instead of pushing them away
- be a success in your own eyes

- study the lives and works of your favorite musicians
- watch the teacher closely
- have a place for everything
- make master lists
- create a safe haven for sleep, rest, and intimacy
- never anticipate wealth from any source but labor
- let go of what cannot be changed
- make wishes for others in a wish fountain
- finish the course
- back up your fresh vegetables with a supply of frozen and canned vegetables
- bring flowers to someone you're picking up at the airport
- embrace change and let go of fear
- give credit to your whole support team
- list ten positive things that happened to you today
- nothing takes the place of persistence
- run your first mile

- win without boasting and lose without excuses
- make use of your mind
- get some depth
- look for beauty in unexpected places
- create a sacred space
- learn to deal with discomfort
- buy a drafting tool for an aspiring architect
- stop spending money frivolously
- laugh at yourself
- give someone a compliment
- accept a breath mint if someone offers you one
- Today isn't any other day, you know (Lewis Carroll)
- save money with integrity
- see discipline as an asset
- notice something that is blossoming today
- avoid repetition
- help children develop a special talent or skill
- eat Rice Krispies instead of a cheeseburger

- increase yang with cereal grains, rice, wheat, legumes, root vegetables, goat cheese, seeds and nuts, meat, eggs, salty fish
- warm someone's cold hands
- learn to work with yourself
- have good manners
- adopt a good habit
- scatter cracked corn for birds during the snowy winter months
- bring appetizers when invited over for cocktails
- treat yourself as you would a special friend
- revel in others' joys
- frame the kids' school pictures
- do great work!
- take part in a St. Patrick's Day parade
- eat a steaming bowl of vegetable soup
- buy a *zafu* (round meditation cushion) from a monastery that will benefit from the purchase

- relish each moment
- do not begrudge others what you cannot enjoy
- obey the law
- love your love handles
- set up a forced savings plan
- replace tired old habits with exciting new ones
- always take ten extra minutes to do something right
- give a cup of tea to the Salvation Army bell ringer
- clean up your school
- inner discipline is doing something simply because you committed yourself to do it
- work for the welfare of others
- plan something pleasant for your morning: homemade muffins, a vase of fresh flowers on the bedside table, Bach's Brandenburg Concertos
- take a winter forest walk and listen for pinecones popping
- downsize without downgrading

- do something nice for someone without letting them know you did it
- ignore the inconsequential
- take time to let the mud in your mind settle
- make Thanksgiving dinner for your in-laws
- let silence empower you
- simply stop talking
- cultivate an awareness of your surroundings
- learn from suffering
- don't say anything about anyone in their absence that you would not say in their presence
- avoid extremes in life; the middle way gives clarity to the mind
- hatha yoga bridges the gap between the sages and modern practice
- open doors for others
- project confidence without being cocky
- find answers to unsolved dilemmas

- put a happy face on your toast with squeeze butter
- offer headphones to someone so he can watch TV or listen to music without disturbing others
- cut yourself some slack
- wear colored Band-Aids
- get along well with others
- make the decision to be happy
- in silence, start to hear your own true voice
- try walking a mile in someone else's shoes
- study psychology
- guard your sleep
- preserve or restore old Christmas tree decorations
- send a fan letter
- do not communicate dissatisfaction with what you are doing at any given moment
- hear all sounds as beautiful music
- write a love letter to each member of your family
- approach love with reckless abandon

- do a seasonal closet cleaning and purge
- deliver birthday breakfasts in bed
- take comfort in the optimism of children
- teach English to a foreigner
- we only have power over our own lives
- be serene in every situation
- let people go ahead of you
- seek out different perspectives when you are faced with an important decision
- feed your brain
- value your humanity over all material things
- write for ten minutes per day about what you have learned from a negative experience
- know when you need more help
- the possibility of transforming ourselves rests in our intentions to awaken
- let employees or students eat or take breaks outdoors when it is nice outside

- find work you love
- clearly define the person you want to be
- pay special attention to the aesthetics of your meal
- Zen archery is a way of moving out of the mind and becoming totally immersed in the movement involved
- embrace your partner often
- trust your common sense and your intuition
- do not allow those who abuse you to affect your mood or spirit
- be respectful of houseguests
- respond from a place of wisdom
- usher in a new age of chivalry
- voluntary simplicity keeps you mindful of what is important
- be inspiring
- don't speak until you have to
- read every day
- cultivate emptiness

- support the Salvation Army and Goodwill
- give cards that "say" something
- make a trip to the library on a gloomy day
- find pleasure in deeper things than profit
- participate in a Toys for Tots program
- learn all you can from failure
- do things for your partner that he or she does not expect
- help someone's ship come in
- build a simple, basic wardrobe
- sharing happiness can become a way of life
- work on being lovable
- develop an astounding appetite for books
- develop a sense of equanimity toward all beings
- wash someone's car
- do the very best you can with what you have
- love the part of you that is growing in attentiveness and the part that does not want to be attentive

- work at liking people and eventually you will like them
- one voice can share wisdom
- live with as much zest as you can muster
- buy shoes that really fit
- return to the Tao
- donate your library to a library
- think things over
- act with composure and mindfulness
- give your mate a pedicure
- have the courage to pay attention to your needs
- think about whether you gossip to avoid real intimacy
- be active rather than reactive
- clean and tune up the kids' bicycles in the spring
- make it your New Year's resolution to accept yourself
- create and maintain a personal support system of friends
- in difficult moments, visualize a favorite place, and transport yourself to that spot

- clean out junk drawers
- patiently focus your mind
- learn to say no to unreasonable requests
- understand yourself, and then you will understand everything
- do a Subway sandwich run for football fans
- help eliminate a cause of poverty in your town
- turn off the telephone, turn on the radio, and hop into a scent-filled tub for one hour
- listen carefully to yourself
- be grateful for a meal, no matter how simple
- enjoy asking questions
- keep criticisms to a minimum
- walk from room to room, making a list of clutter areas to clear out
- rent a rowboat on a nearby lake
- when the student is ready, the teacher will appear
- practice the art of remembering names

- go out and look at the stars to put things in perspective
- rise earlier than the others
- volunteer at the headquarters of a political candidate
- just see, just do
- stay curious, explore, discover
- resolve your past karma
- remove the suffering and you are left with happiness
- use soft cloths and nice-smelling cleaning products
- if you are fully present in the moment, time will be suspended
- rise above the confines of individualistic concerns
- mist the indoor plants
- be aware of your impulses toward greed
- continuously work on your unfinished business
- if it looks fun and it does not break the Ten Commandments, do it
- get rid of things on a regular basis

- repeat, "Where am I? Here. What time is it? Now."
- talk late into the night when someone needs it
- have a picnic by a lake
- eat food that pleases all your senses
- give a computer to a college-bound kid
- this moment is the perfect moment to let go
- increase your awareness of how you hold your body
- cheer on working women
- relax and be yourself
- take sensible action
- acknowledge the truth of your dissatisfaction
- real power comes in complete calmness
- accomplish what you undertake
- work a crossword puzzle
- take real lunch breaks
- endear yourself to others by not strutting your stuff
- meditate in the late afternoon to allow unconscious material to erupt

- make sure kids have lots of paints
- be the place where the good times are
- before getting out of bed, consciously relax and take ten deep breaths
- catalog your lifetime of acquired talents, from childhood knowledge to adult challenges
- increase yang by doing strength training and aerobics, meditating midday, rising early, spending a lot of time outdoors
- the truth of Zen can turn one's life into art
- get a massage from a certified massage therapist
- live life spontaneously
- carry water with you wherever you go
- spread joy to others
- maintain integrity
- notice when someone changes her appearance or hair
- when you stop blaming others, you regain your sense of personal power

- let opposition strengthen your resolve
- make sure the way to your front door is well-lighted
- be thankful that you can appreciate whatever the day will bring
- use nonjudgmental, meditative awareness to help open your mind
- Out of clutter; find simplicity. From discord, find harmony. In the middle of difficulty lies opportunity (Albert Einstein)
- never expect to lose
- rearrange a room for better flow
- relax hundreds of muscles in your face by smiling
- know that this is a wonderful moment
- don't keep your appreciation of details to yourself
- know the signs of overtraining for a sport
- look at your life like a creative process
- take someone dancing
- get to know yourself better

- if circumstances are bad, do not make them a part of yourself
- when you notice that you are pushing yourself to complete a task, soften and be merciful with yourself
- say, "I am balanced, calm, and serene"
- confront calamity
- respect the right of others to be different
- ask questions
- do the laundry for someone else who always does it
- get out of the got-to-tell-all, lay-it-on-the-line syndrome
- everything is the same; nothing is wrong, nothing is right
- avoid eating between meals
- after you have hit bottom, find things to be happy about
- purchase turkeys for a food bank
- educate kids about the importance of preserving the earth and the environment

- eat enough to fill emptiness and maintain energy
- put a huge smile on jack-o'-lanterns
- reduce clutter — it detracts from the flow of energy
- begin any communication in a friendly way
- live life as a today rather than a yesterday or a tomorrow
- wake up happy
- fear nobody and nothing; that which is the most precious in you cannot be damaged by anyone or anything
- a wind chime in a window keeps the energy in
- delight in your children
- recognize mere appearances for what they are
- have a very good time
- leave a note of appreciation for someone who has a beautiful garden
- schedule exercise in red pen
- plan ahead

- take time to dream
- be the neighbor who comes to help at the slightest hint of trouble
- look ahead when entering a room
- read a joke book
- surrender to the now
- buy things that require low levels of maintenance
- get a child his first fish tank
- don't accept any abuse, anger, or threat
- make an uplifting quotation book for someone
- nonviolence requires much more courage than violence
- buy from neighborhood kids for their fund-raisers
- imagine yourself as an artist when you cook
- probe the depths of experience
- read things that require effort, thought, and concentration
- make your anniversary an all-day event

- practice patriotism
- be mindful of the quality and quantity of food you eat
- help someone with a crossword puzzle
- touch a face with your eyes closed
- when life is very rough, be very calm and the way
  will become clear
- moonlight because you want to
- know that every moment is unrepeatable and sacred
- simplicity is having room for the unexpected
- put night lights about so no one goes bump in
  the night
- increase your playfulness quotient
- the method is mindfulness, the expression is
  compassion, and the essence is wisdom
- take time to talk to a friend's child who is thinking
  about a career in your field
- write a book that changes someone's life for the better
- practice purposeful relaxation

- find a way to work with difficulties
- see the work you do as spiritual practice
- pay your fair share
- make use of anything life happens to bring your way
- don't nag others to change
- be humble
- perceive the divine mystery of things
- earn the approval of honest critics
- don't give up on someone, even when the person lets you down
- have a simple meal, take a simple walk, perform a simple chore without hurrying
- accept the day's weather
- groom yourself like a racehorse
- self-restraint, consideration for others, politeness, fairness, generosity, and tact all enrich and ennoble human life
- gladden the heart of a child

- learn a variety of relaxation techniques and practice at least one regularly
- burn red, blue, or purple candles to stimulate fame, fortune, reputation, happiness, festivity
- baby-sit for free
- take a deep breath and tell the truth
- go to an exercise class
- give away your hope chest to a bride-to-be
- live Zen: let go of your perception of need
- cultivate a love for home life
- choose your thoughts carefully
- sit with a Buddhist group in your area, or sit at a local silent Quaker meeting
- when you review your day and hit a memory that evokes an emotion, pause, evaluate it, and rectify it if necessary
- put a tiny plant on a friend's windowsill
- allow yourself and others to be silent

- know what you want
- donate a teddy bear to a children's hospital
- acceptance is an act of pure grace; acceptance is the opposite of judgment
- think of yourself as a survivor
- go outside and clear your mind
- support a ban on smoking in public places
- take slow deep breaths while on the phone, in the car, or while waiting
- relinquish the illusory notion of being in charge
- hug someone tight and whisper, "I love you"
- watch what you say
- keep a statue of the Buddha nearby
- stop overscheduling
- when there is anger, offer loving-kindness
- sing in the shower or chant on the street if that's what you feel like doing
- appreciate a caring doctor

- work toward goals
- be friends with good-natured people
- for ten minutes, jot down your thoughts and associations as they occur
- do less arguing and more forgiving
- share popcorn at the movies
- ease spinal tension and improve your balance with the Rolling-Like-a-Ball pose (curl up and hold your legs) eases spinal tension and helps your balance
- spend at least one hour a week with each child doing a favorite activity
- prefer to have less
- ask yourself what you teach your children that they will eventually have to unlearn
- focus on building a strong center
- allow enough time for unhurried cooking and eating
- your problems are not caused by some other person or a difficult situation, but by how you perceive them

 273 instant karma

- downsize, so that you can support your lifestyle with work you enjoy
- do not be envious, deceitful, or greedy
- make a milkshake for someone who is feeling down
- *vata* types need to introduce and maintain regularity in their lives
- deal with mistakes and mix-ups early
- teach a kid how to fix and maintain a car
- bend over backwards
- explore every winding path
- use less and share more
- kiss your mom, hug your dad
- pay your parking tickets
- focus on the world's hope rather than the world's tragedies
- listen carefully to criticism
- consider nurturing foster children
- look up instead of down

- take a vacation in your own backyard
- praise others
- attach a love note to the steering wheel
- The practice is the teacher. Your practice is your teacher. (Maurine Stuart)
- take nothing for granted
- escape complacency
- remove your own impurities little by little
- leave a goody basket at the apartment of a shut-in
- the wise don't need to prove their point
- have a heart
- develop a sense of responsibility based on altruism
- volunteer for an archaeological dig
- have team spirit
- never speak loudly to each other, unless the house is on fire
- have a simple, direct message on your answering machine

- give someone a chance to sleep in
- be a chaperone on field trips
- sit down when you eat
- give someone a brand-new book, hot off the press
- learn to be in the world with a quiet mind
- offer someone your chair or seat
- live in gratitude
- run for political office
- practice conservation ecology
- it is never too late
- be aware of the passing of time and yet the timelessness of each moment
- close generation gaps
- value leisure
- your teacher can open the door, but you must enter by yourself
- lie with your legs raised against a wall to unkink your mind and body

instant karma 276

- think noble thoughts
- plant daffodil bulbs for naturalizing the garden
- keep promises to yourself
- drink cranberry juice regularly
- kiss your loved ones good night
- to understand your mind, you must watch it while it is angry, while it desires, while it is in conflict
- appreciate an idyllic quiet
- keep a journal of ridiculous things that happen to you
- live a humble life
- there are no coincidences
- trust in your own inherent goodness
- learn the trade, not the "tricks" of the trade
- leave spaces in your day to do something spontaneous
- provide direction and vision to others
- resist restocking after you clear out your clutter
- have true, lasting values
- help if it is in your power to do so

 instant karma

- help regulate your metabolism with regular stretching and gentle exercise in the morning
- volunteer for beach cleanup
- borrow a friend's child for a few hours to allow your friend an afternoon off
- train wholeheartedly
- break a wishbone with someone you love and wish that their dream comes true
- put stuff away
- work toward a peaceful and civilized world
- do something fun
- take a single sacred breath to clear the body and mind of momentary grasping
- treat your listeners with courtesy and respect
- give your in-laws framed photos of the family
- fill salads with lots of different-colored vegetables
- practice making healthier choices
- know how to work the circuit breaker

- say to yourself, "I have the ability, I have the determination, I shall succeed"
- date foods you put into the freezer
- be less bothered by the actions of others
- find fulfillment in daily activities
- learn as much from your kids as they learn from you
- own less
- begin to see how you are caught by attachment
- demonstrate a commitment to compassion
- smile at someone who never smiles at you
- light cypress or cedar in an incense burner
- stay away from alcoholic drinks
- do what fulfills you, even if you are not paid to do it
- return something loaned to you by a friend
- write poetry as an exercise of self-discovery
- use what you have rather than buy new things
- stretch
- clear garden debris so plants can grow

- aim for quality
- realize how important it is to be a child
- strive, persist — then relax
- join the Peace Corps and teach basic business or household skills
- inner freedom comes from seeing what is true
- give someone a jar of olives as a symbol of peacemaking
- eat in order to maintain strength and prolong your life, not merely to satisfy hunger
- respect differences
- follow your heart
- make up your mind to be happy
- buy Chanel No. 5 cologne for your mom
- Do what you can, with what you have, where you are (Theodore Roosevelt)
- if you're going to consume happiness, produce happiness

- find alternatives to wearing fur
- take others seriously
- make some quiet time to let negative emotions subside
- send small gifts to brighten a long day
- get out of your box
- make happiness mandatory and misery optional
- limit your requirements
- attend to your own business
- share your time and your possessions
- appreciate the contagious energy and excitement of children
- the worst could happen or the best could happen, but often it's somewhere in between
- give yourself permission to abandon any activity midway when you need to
- spiritual riches matter more than material riches
- maintain mental purity and physical cleanliness
- allow your facial muscles to be soft

- offer to be on the cleanup committee
- find the good in everyone
- teach your children good work ethics
- let someone who usually prepares breakfast stay in bed
- make one change at a time
- give the gift of communication
- twice a day, stop the world
- learn to use Chinese therapy cloisonné balls
  for massage
- love each day equally
- communicate your needs, ideas, and opinions in
  a positive way
- know the power of a generous heart
- avoid taking other people's inventory
- think of unusual strategies
- listen to what your dreams tell you
- practice navigating through all the ups and downs
  you encounter

- acknowledge the connection of all beings
- change one thing — start immediately,
  do it flamboyantly, make no exceptions
- preserve nature
- Let go of all content and you will be totally content
  (Bernard Gunther)
- donate a ten-gallon jug of fruit salad to a senior center
- keep fresh vegetables, washed and cut up,
  in bags in the fridge
- let someone know that you are thinking about
  him or her
- use the freshest, best-quality ingredients possible
- live for other people
- have a cup personalized for a child
- be a voracious reader
- safeguard your privacy
- clean up after yourself
- give up something that is not good for you

- explore what you like to do
- your religion should be kindness
- spend time pursuing your own hobbies: cooking, gardening, writing
- stand tall, even in the face of opposition
- make allowances
- give in to neither passion nor sadness
- view all problems as opportunities to learn and grow
- share food with others
- A wise man makes more opportunities than he finds (Francis Bacon)
- watch Saturday morning cartoons as a family
- you save time by taking your time
- be prepared
- study uplifting verses of scripture
- create your own personal prayer book
- the next time you feel something is missing or not quite right, turn inward and just sit

- earn the respect of colleagues
- honesty is good for your health
- the best food is the food you make
- ask your mate to be your exercise partner
- when you listen to someone, give up all your subjective opinions
- arrange for your family to spend a day together: watch old movies, collaborate on the crossword puzzle, exchange stories, order in pizza
- take care of little things — they can make big improvements
- own your textbooks
- know your limits
- make every day Valentine's Day
- arrange to go on a hot-air balloon ride
- throw an end-of-season party for a team
- take a "brain break" of ten minutes every hour
- hang up your coat or jacket when you come in

- let everything disappear into the background of your mind
- allow plenty of time to get places
- take care of what you have
- refrain from speaking about an absent third person
- be partners with someone
- stop analyzing or trying to figure out other people
- reclaim your time
- plans and ideas are fine — it is the attachment to these ideas that cause trouble
- when you hear or read a new word or phrase, look it up and make a note of it
- laughter is good for the soul
- appreciate the moment of arrival
- try things on for size mentally
- you'll get more with honey than vinegar
- one handclasp can lift a soul
- know the astronauts' names

- meditate upon how it is the hub or center of the wheel that holds the rest of the wheel together and influences its direction and speed
- take a quiet walk when you feel like blowing your top
- post report cards and special awards on the fridge
- take a ten-minute rest, wrapped in a terry robe
- discover and like your child's opinions
- practice *ujjayi* breath to cool the head: breathe with your lips closed, making sounds like Darth Vader
- exude a quiet confidence
- say, "Have a nice day" to the checkout person
- apologize immediately when you lose your temper
- use your enthusiasm to put yourself in forward gear
- try to recognize small problems as beneficial
- let speakers finish their own sentences
- learn the secret of getting along with people
- chew well to strengthen your teeth, their roots, and your gums

- buy wool socks for a hiker or backpacker
- buy pizza for a group of teens who are hanging out
- be aware of life's possibilities
- eat especially healthfully today
- experiment with new ways of thinking
- grant employees leave when needed
- have an intimate talk with your mother
- imagine yourself blowing an urge away like smoke
- unconditionally outlaw lying in your relationships
- have patience with all things, but chiefly with yourself
- work diligently
- recognize that you can control your thoughts
- stretch your wings
- recognize that what you think is what you are
- pamper yourself and a friend with pedicures
- your garden is a microcosm of the world
- brainstorm chore ideas for children
- take a moral inventory of your life

- thank all of your best teachers
- aim for only one to two pounds of weight loss per week
- pay close attention
- have something bright yellow in your office
- start a community quilt project to raise money for a good cause
- patronize "off the beaten track" establishments
- however many holy words you read, however many you speak, what good will they do if you do not act upon them?
- raise your consciousness
- say thank you as often as possible
- celebrate half-birthdays
- say grace
- stop nagging the kids at the dinner table
- live, don't just exist
- eat one meal with earplugs and listen to the sound of feasting

- volunteer to help coach a junior sports team
- display school spirit
- give a small dinner party to celebrate friends
- see a counselor or spiritual leader if you are having great difficulties
- start to believe in what you want
- serve the common good
- make solitude a celebration
- give yourself the freedom to write, to walk, to wander
- at least once each day, try to listen to others without judgment
- take advantage of those moments when you feel naturally meditative
- bake blueberry muffins on a Saturday morning
- make creative and well-prepared lunches
- volunteer for Head Start
- buy an outrageous banana split for a child who makes the honor roll

- choose comfort over fashion
- look for the lessons others have to teach you
- learn to find joy in everything you do
- be a role model for a younger person
- be persistent
- take a few minutes at the end of your working day to close your eyes and find your inner peace
- get involved in charitable projects
- play inspiring music
- push nagging thoughts out of your head
- transform chores into meditation by establishing and maintaining awareness while doing them
- write a letter to your son or daughter at college
- make note of the good things that happen to you during the day
- buy several pairs of winter gloves and give them to needy people
- converse with your Higher Power

- embrace and support your body, with all its faults
- assess what works, but don't blame yourself for what does not
- wear a totally outrageous outfit
- share sandwich crusts with animals
- console a crying baby
- fight disease — through education, service, fund-raising
- go on a vision quest: venture alone into the wilderness for a few days, fasting and meditating
- dare to experiment with your own life
- use the resources at hand to create something new
- each day, commit a selfless act that no one else knows about
- frame a child's painting
- reach out in kindness when those around you are difficult
- thank the friend who introduced you to Mr. Right

- hold on to the center
- recognize and honor your happy self and inner spirit
- people-watch at a busy boardwalk or mall
- take a box of used toys to the homeless shelter
- change with the seasons
- find a quiet refuge outdoors where you can gather your thoughts
- drop thoughts of greed or hate
- cut back on commitments when you need a break
- draw the letters *I-L-O-V-E-Y-O-U* on someone's back or arm with your finger
- delegate, but do not dump, tasks to others
- don't be a slave to the telephone
- stop counting chickens before they are hatched
- give because you want to touch someone
- say only nice things to yourself
- Sometimes the highest form of action is inaction (Jerry Brown)

- do your own landscaping with the help of library books
- listen to a teacher's suggestions and guidance
- sign up for a big-league baseball camp for adults
- secure a reprieve from life's pressures
- passively witness the sensations associated with the in-breath
- meditate as you walk
- resolve not to eat when standing or walking
- acknowledge that there is room for growth
- let a pet soak up your warmth
- leave food unwrapped in the refrigerator to preserve the food's *chi*
- reserve a window table for a special meal
- savor the importance of ritual meals: Thanksgiving, Passover, Easter, Christmas
- anger makes a groove in the mind that allows more anger to arise easily
- participate in a new activity at least once a week

- reach for that which you consider difficult and make it possible
- bring orange slices for the soccer team
- hand down a two-generation cookbook
- take the time to experience something sweet at the moment it is in front of you
- do three to eleven minutes of alternate leg lifts, lying flat on your back, for strength
- A merry heart doeth thee good like medicine (Proverbs)
- show patience with problems
- Get rid of the self, and act from the self (Zen saying)
- hang wind chimes where you can hear them
- take brain breaks
- fix a leaky toilet or faucet
- use your greatest talent
- buy a disposable camera for a child about to go on vacation

- allow everything to be as it is
- take the extra minute to notice
- excel at helping others excel
- go a whole day without becoming angry
- plant a tree
- do this pre-sleep relaxation: lie on your back and breathe through your nose, the exhalation twice as long as the inhalation
- take part in eclectic activities
- clean up after your pets
- engage in rewarding, relaxing hobbies or other interests
- place a quarter in the coin return of a pay phone
- use your library for enriching cultural activities — music, meditation, art, or reading
- sit up straight in movies, chairs, cars, and airplanes
- order extra Girl Scout cookies to give to others
- give a teenager tickets to a special sporting event

- help those affected by natural disasters
- take good care of the ones you love
- treasure time like gold
- remember that mindfulness is portable and invisible
- go through an attic's forgotten curios with your grandmother
- work at home one or more days a week if possible
- specially decorate family birthday cakes
- promote the creation of a local bike path
- make time and space for an intuitive leap
- enjoy a good yawn
- bring the paper to someone who needs a rest
- give the gift of time, energy, or creativity
- in the light of awareness, habit falls away
- send flowers to your child's day-care provider
- become more interested in understanding others than being understood
- express glee

- undertake for one week not to speak about anyone who is not present
- in order to keep everything, you have to be willing to let go of everything
- if it will brighten someone's day, say it
- give a senior a gift certificate for a cleaning service
- be happy with the way you look
- vow not to engage in sexual misconduct
- return kind words for negative as often as possible
- substitute wholesome thoughts for unwholesome ones
- The road is better than the inn (Miguel de Cervantes)
- finish the laundry for someone
- try to achieve perfect balance in tai chi
- live within your income
- remember how much more important people are to you than the issue that is bothering you
- Life is a mystery to be lived, not a problem to be solved (Zen saying)

- learn how to relax the body and mind rapidly, thoroughly, and at will to deepen the beneficial effects of yoga *asanas* (poses)
- empty yourself of greed and grasping desire, the root of all suffering
- be willing to learn from different perspectives
- take a child out for a day of fun
- accept authority that is legal and ethical
- practice showing your best self
- join your company's wellness program
- celebrate the accomplishments of others
- put your important documents in a safe-deposit box
- bring doughnuts or bagels and cream cheese for the whole office
- see your mistakes as learning opportunities
- make peace with the fact that some of the best people in your life are fallible, unreasonable, and sometimes downright annoying

- everything is moving at the proper speed
- keep the spark of adventure alive
- encourage a kid to stay in school
- use a mandala for concentration when you begin to meditate
- spend the week before Christmas as a Salvation Army bell ringer
- in conflict, be fair and generous
- rejoice in change
- wear a bike helmet when you go for a ride
- eat dark chocolate
- pack your own lunch
- foster a child's awareness that happiness and satisfaction come from inside
- do things slowly instead of in a hurry
- have sunny thoughts on cloudy days
- deal with overpowering ill will by generating loving thoughts

instant karma 300

- push back the sheets and jump out of bed
- appreciate a cardinal's brilliance against the snow
- drink deeply from the well of life
- if one has a sense of contentment and simplicity, that's enough
- teach at a religious camp
- set aside a grudge
- serve yourself without feeling guilty
- forgo the frivolous and embrace what counts
- reread specific passages and chapters when seeking inspiration
- teach a child about your favorite hobby
- make a quiet spot for someone to study
- see beyond the obvious
- nothing can bring you peace but yourself
- be frugal
- be a living expression of kindness
- love powerfully

- think of something likable about the person you dislike the most
- help achieve racial harmony
- you create your reality with your thoughts and intentions
- believe that life was given for joy
- let a convenient parking space go to someone else
- think like Leonardo da Vinci
- live like a child
- only by starting where you are can you ever get anywhere
- give in occasionally for someone you love
- the point of meditation is learning the difference between thinking and being lost in thought
- when you do general chakra meditation, notice the vibrancy of each color; if any seem dull, there may be a problem to address in that energy center
- remain centered in a moment of stress

- celebrate the harvest moon by taking a long stroll with someone special after dinner
- become aware of your inner energy through the Zen technique of circular breathing
- use your best china
- ride on Ferris wheels that come into your area
- find a doctor who is a good listener
- write your child's teacher a note of appreciation
- there is a reason for everything
- support solutions to clean up the world's dumping grounds
- have thirty minutes or so of unstructured time every day to do something new
- sit down for your meals
- feel for others as you do for yourself
- get the cobwebs out of your head
- stop rushing around, sit quietly, switch off the world, and come back to the earth

 instant karma

- play morning music
- develop relationships that go beyond color, race, religion, and politics
- offer Life Savers or Pez to someone who's feeling down
- create routines that soothe the soul
- say something nice to someone
- sit on the steps and wait for your child to come home
- seek homeopathic remedies for an illness
- drink responsibly
- vote in every election
- make sure your kids have a safe place to hang out
- put an altar in the northwest part of the house or a room, or in a room across from the front door
- always breathe through the nose unless you have an allergy, cold, or sinus problem
- compliment everyone you deal with
- loosen your grip on what is always changing, let go of struggle, and let go of suffering

instant karma 304

- buy surprise books for kids
- make some progress every single day
- redefine wealth to mean "having enough"
- use a kaleidoscope
- accomplish small tasks as if they were great and noble
- purify vices
- understand how your food and lifestyle affect
  your physical and mental health
- turn disappointments into discoveries
- set the highest possible goals for yourself
- get cordless phones for elderly people
- think of yourself as a programmable computer
- let go of any anger or resentment you hold toward
  someone who helped sow the seeds of your bad habit
- have the kindness to tolerate others' mistakes
- use plant-based, nonpetrochemical cleansers
  for your body and home
- eat till you're satisfied — not a bite more

- install carbon monoxide and smoke detectors in your grandparents' house
- keep your car for as long as you can
- go up to the attic and try to throw away ten things bigger than a breadbox
- return library books promptly
- leave a funny card under a windshield wiper
- share your lap with a cat
- don't compare or envy
- honor your peers
- when you are starting something new and challenging, do not be afraid of being afraid
- go somewhere you have never been
- take a picnic and enjoy the sunset
- be of good cheer
- have a healthy respect for the unknown
- try to deal skillfully with problems as they arise
- take a friend grocery shopping

- ride a bicycle with a child
- instead of assuming, ask
- tap your own maple trees and make your own syrup
- take an aunt to lunch
- be like an island that no flood can engulf
- experience the relief of being out of the grip of a craving
- do not eat when you are angry
- thinking about your goals will bring you closer to them
- remember that religion is personal
- celebrate a friend's fifteen minutes of fame
- cushion your work schedule with breaks
- accept your flaws with the same grace and humility as your best qualities
- **remember birthdays**
- do not believe in something solely because someone has told you so
- see, hear, taste, feel, smell

- don't give up just because of the length of time it will take to accomplish a dream
- do something about your annoying habits
- build a dollhouse for a little girl
- if you cling to nothing, you can handle anything
- develop compassion for all living beings
- use your lunch hour productively
- wave to the crosswalk patrol
- practice putting your own feelings and judgments aside when you listen to others
- what do you truly need in order to be happy?
- give tender, loving touches
- remember there is no such thing as "mine"
- practice reflexology to restore energy
- have the courage to swallow your pride
- try to look into the eyes and heart of each person you meet
- finish projects ahead of deadline

- buy a big bouquet and give a flower to each person who looks like they could use it
- share silence
- give a pet some love
- do a rise-and-shine stretch
- expect more from yourself than anyone else expects of you
- share with others whatever experiences of beauty and pleasure you have
- edit and control less; appreciate more
- say yes to something today that you would usually say no to
- make sure your résumé calls attention to your natural talents
- when you are flat broke, lend money to a dear friend who is down and out
- give teenagers gift certificates so they can pick out their own presents

- say "good morning," even if it isn't
- volunteer at the local nursing home
- rise above objects of desire
- help someone dig a garden
- bake cookies for someone who can't
- remember that you have the ability to start over
- read a book by a stream
- teach your kids how to use appliances correctly
- correct your children's behavior in private
- make food from scratch whenever possible
- always smell clean
- sweet-talk yourself into a lull
- surprise your partner and pick him or her up from work
- choose to live the life that you have now
- be quiet and let your actions speak for you
- throw back the catch of the day
- buy in bulk and use coupons

- let someone else go first
- frame an important document for someone
- reacquire the courage of a child
- open a nearby window to let in the sounds and smells of the season
- get as much sunshine per day as you can
- make copies of home movies to send to relatives
- let people know where they stand with you
- renew your love
- let reality be the teacher
- give others ample opportunity to speak
- refuse to feel humiliation
- observe the relationship between thoughts and actions
- keep Christmas enjoyable by toning it down
- do not wish for gratitude
- recognize that the other person is you
- There is nothing that will not reveal its secrets if you love it enough (George Washington Carver)

- watch your breath as you get into a comfortable sleeping position
- don't struggle unduly to make things happen the way you want them to
- making something hard never makes it better — it just makes it hard
- practice mental alertness
- define exactly what you want to accomplish in detail
- sponsor a block-party potluck
- appreciate Yankee ingenuity
- get a parrot and teach it happy words and phrases
- make up after a fight
- adopt an acre of rain forest
- set up a scholarship fund
- be authentic
- be the friend of all living things
- when you score a base hit, don't wish it were a home run

- enjoy the sitcom of your life without being overwhelmed by the melodramatic moments
- send a telegram to someone you love
- take a sick day when you are sick
- eschew diets
- accept what comes your way without doubt and without fear
- be of benefit to others
- train yourself to be a listener
- accept problems as an inevitable part of life
- make a surprise breakfast in bed for someone
- first improve what's easiest to improve
- establish a mentor program
- win and lose graciously
- find out what you are really meant to do
- give Grandma a spa vacation
- do the right thing, regardless of what others think
- spend happy hours organizing things in the attic

- If you truly love yourself, you would never harm another (Buddha)
- introduce yourself to a neighbor you have never met
- compliment your server
- if you snore, find a way to stop
- rub a dog's belly
- you won't find what you are looking for at the mall
- see things for what they really are
- drive smart
- rid yourself of debt
- cleanse your inner vision until you see the light
- make a commitment
- discover the power of self-forgiveness
- recognize that words are imperfect, so give them limited importance
- make the present count for everything; right now is your only life
- get ready for death by living a good life

- display the things you love
- inquire/listen/learn
- ask someone to the Sadie Hawkins dance
- put a red carpet in the bedroom to bring good fortune and happiness
- pay attention to the things that are working positively in your life
- enjoy a special time with your child
- try alternate nostril breathing to calm, balance, and regulate energy
- plan a baby or wedding shower for a best friend
- throw out old shoes that you never wear anymore
- avoid white poisons like sugar, salt, and white flour
- acknowledge someone's accomplishment
- find a mentor
- acknowledge your ability to learn intuitively
- go sailing and feel the wind on your face
- bring fresh air into the house whenever you can

315 instant karma

- deal with mistakes openly and fairly
- ask for help if you need it
- use your words to convey patience
- help heal someone's soul
- dismantle piles of things
- open children's eyes to the needs and rights of others
- what really matters is what you do with what you have
- look at each tabletop as a still life
- send grandparents recent school and sports pictures
- touch the earth
- accept yourself as you are, right now
- see opinions forming and melting away like snowflakes
- stand up for a friend
- choose to value things that are within your grasp
- study in a northeast area of your home
- focus on what you feed your mind
- know that a geographic escape takes you nowhere
- appreciate happy unplanned moments

- credit your source of inspiration
- discreetly remove your shoes when sitting on an airplane or a train
- learn how to respond quietly
- lead as you would like to be led
- let someone make you laugh
- remember that most of the time, the worst does not happen
- strengthen your immune system by laughing
- choose to be alone rather than be with those who will hinder your progress
- support everybody's right to enjoy democracy
- practice qigong to stimulate the circulation of *chi* throughout the body and promote self-healing
- encourage kids to cooperate
- look people in the eye
- realize that when you are happy, you are in touch with your greatest human potential

- make molehills out of mountains
- trust your intuition to guide your decisions
- avoid things that cause harm
- vote for higher education budgets
- relieve your feet by running them over a zippered plastic bag of ice cubes and water
- have good, clean fun
- love charitable acts for the happiness they bring to others
- a good traveler has no fixed plans and is not intent upon arriving
- be one with the creative intelligence of the universe
- tell others about kindnesses you have experienced
- see yourself as a work in progress
- learn by the experiences, examples, and writings of others
- break down tasks into smaller tasks
- believe people tell the truth

- wave to the highway patrolman with the radar
- read while you wait
- tip your hat to show respect or admiration
- upon waking, take three deep, mindful breaths
- respect someone else's individuality and capacity for growth
- realize that mistakes can be corrected
- frame an old map for a history buff
- give narcissus, plum blossoms, hyacinths, and orchids as gifts for Chinese New Year
- avoid *tamasic* foods (meat, alcohol, onions, garlic; fermented, stale, overripe foods), which promote lethargy, laziness, and inactivity
- plan days with no conversation, only contemplation
- think the truth, tell the truth, live the truth
- do your job well
- ignore media messages
- assign work that is manageable

- be grateful for the future possibilities that await you
- travel by bicycle
- eat the healthiest food, live in the healthiest environment, have the healthiest attitude and lifestyle
- do something each day for someone who will never be able to repay you
- do something to kick yourself out of unproductive doldrums
- take action
- clean out the medicine cabinet
- refrain from actions that create confusion
- welcome everything that happens to you
- donate books to a school library
- help children solve their own problems
- look at life as an adventure
- disengage from your mind
- thank those who have given to you
- overcome your doubts and fears

- ask yourself, "Is this task or behavior really necessary or is it just a way to be busy?"
- set reasonable parameters for yourself
- work for peace in every possible way
- sit in a dark room with just one candle
- practice doing less but enjoying it more
- if your mind is talking, don't take it personally
- become aware of the fear that is influencing you
- follow Gandhi's ethic of passive resistance
- listen closely to the advice of loved ones
- learn how to manage your own stress
- buy biodegradable products from companies that do not test on animals
- make sponge or color-blot paintings with your kids
- don't steal your child's chance to do something on his own by doing it for him
- make warm winter meals
- savor the sensual experience of eating

- keep socially active
- the best motivation for meditation is to live to your full potential and to benefit others (the bodhisattva ideal)
- begin each day with your favorite music
- the trouble is that you think you have time
- give your best, then let the rest be given to you
- keep food safe to eat
- set an example
- balance your work with fun
- buy land/open space to save it from development
- let your life be a story worth telling right now
- clean out your closet
- imagine all the useful information we could accumulate over a lifetime by keeping an open mind
- rid yourself of the *chi* of your busy day by taking a shower or bath
- use your creativity to adapt and compromise
- let go of your opinions

- make a gigantic banner for someone's birthday
- you will never be asked to cope with more than you can handle
- better to do nothing than to do harm
- wake up ten minutes before the rest of the family to practice some yoga
- encourage the work of others
- learn from history
- practice self-acceptance
- get to the office first and make a pot of coffee
- believe in what you're about to do
- put a plant in the windowsill for peace
- to harvest food and to eat is a celebration of the interconnection of all life
- let someone else have the last word
- respectfully pay attention to yourself
- share your feelings with loved ones
- treat every person with dignity and grace

 instant karma

- use artful foods presented artfully; they feed us in more ways than one
- buy fresh foods grown locally and organically
- don't let concern with what other people think dictate your life
- slow down — begin an activity with one gentle inhalation and a calm exhalation
- in the evening, eat as little as possible
- read everything on the summer reading list
- write a thank you to the local peace officers
- expect things to go right
- act with courtesy and fairness regardless of how others treat you
- look for many solutions
- vary your yoga routine
- clean your home regularly to revitalize *chi* energy
- sweat
- take part in informative conversations

- love every man because God loves every man
- appreciate the gentle sounds of a summer Sunday
- take a child to visit a TV studio
- nonviolent thoughts are as important as nonviolent words; let your negative thoughts go
- think quietly
- develop a genuine interest in others' work and hobbies
- be easy to speak to
- cease doing something as soon as you see that it is wrong
- observe etiquette
- true self-esteem can be obtained only through living in balance
- leave secret love notes hidden all over
- notice when your child does something right
- live as if you are on vacation — savoring every minute and collecting memories like snapshots
- create delightful rooms for children

- push sad memories away from you
- offer gratitude for all the things you have experienced
- dream about things you need to resolve
- get rid of anger or restlessness just by acknowledging it
- trust in your ability to come up with new ways of seeing
- heal an old hurt, forgive an old offense
- offer a kid a summer job
- schedule alternate activities to TVs and computers
- plant a seed and watch it grow
- we can't have everything, but we can point ourselves in the right direction
- volunteer as a firefighter
- let nature be your teacher
- eat your biggest meal at lunch and you will increase your energy during the day
- finish that project you left hanging
- keep learning
- give poinsettias to a nursing home

instant karma

- remember that cravings stop going where they are not fed
- write a love poem or letter from the bottom of your heart
- only a quiet mind can learn
- close, don't slam, doors behind you
- read Mary Engelbreit's books
- grow as your love grows
- see that there is a way to go inside
- note how a cloud passing in front of the sun can refresh your mood
- follow tasks through to completion
- campaign for universal, subsidized higher education
- find the courage to change your beliefs when they no longer fit the person you have become
- be aware of your personal behavior
- tell good news to others
- rotate food choices to lessen their accumulative effect

 instant karma

- bring beauty and meaning into life
- live life as a play
- organize a neighborhood picnic
- decide to make a difference
- jump rope
- cleanse a person's energy by tracing her body, head to toe, with a bell
- have a first-aid book on hand
- the way to be happy is to make others so
- get your mind off your own ego
- learn to be grateful and yet not expect too much from others
- life and happiness are driven from the inside out
- say, "Nice doggie"
- learn the origins of words
- think of yourself as a student
- watch a flower slowly open its petals
- give chicken soup to a friend who is under the weather

- be one with the *sangha* (community of believers)
- enjoy your own creativity
- treat an injury early and comprehensively
- base your purchases and financial investments
  on corporate social responsibility
- It is better to light one small candle than to curse
  the darkness (Confucius)
- play a card game with the seniors at the senior center
- awaken someone with a kiss
- do things you are good at
- never tire of helping others
- meditate in the bathtub
- drink lemonade on warm summer nights
- thank someone for great advice
- support medical research
- do ordinary stuff in an extraordinary way
- befriend who you really are
- read works by the world's greatest philosophers

- settle your differences
- accept a compliment
- maximize your life's harmony with nature
- listen to nothing; it is more intriguing than listening for something
- go to bed early, wake up early
- welcome change with grace and humor
- make amends for thoughts, words, and actions you recognize as wrong
- call a friend and ask them out for an ice cream on the spur of the moment
- send a little surprise to someone's hotel
- say you are sorry when you hurt somebody
- put a crystal in a window if the view includes anything unpleasant
- give big applause to small achievements
- *kapha* types should make deliberate changes to their routine to keep from getting in a rut

- celebrate a mother's quiet acts of love
- begin your day in acceptance and thankfulness
- celebrate new babies
- whatever you give you will receive, but you cannot possess what you take
- let a child set the table
- make a graduation quilt out of a child's old T-shirts
- set a good example
- if you cannot pronounce the ingredients listed on a package of food, do not eat it
- enjoy a crackling fire and soft music
- give yourself a facial
- be prepared to practice meditation for a lifetime
- adopt a baseball team of "hard-to-place" children
- practice self-control
- improve your vocabulary
- The best way out is always through (Robert Frost)
- invest yourself in good work

 instant karma

- know your limits: how much sleep you need, how much downtime you need, how many changes you are capable of making at any given time
- learn to live an intentional life rather than an "accidental" life
- choose what you will do, feel, and think
- always be truthful, especially with a child
- plan special times as if they were summits
- serve breakfast or brunch to someone you love
- play board games instead of video games
- discover harmony in all things
- an antidote to restlessness is concentration — count breaths to ten, then start again
- in winter, put up the storm sashes, check the woodpile, and make sure the oil tank is full
- reach out to a deprived child
- immerse yourself in the atmosphere of long walks
- embrace every minute

- learn from mistakes
- lighten up on those closest to you
- campaign against cellular phone use in cars and inappropriate places
- imagine that you have permission to be happy and to really enjoy your life
- chew well and slowly to bring a whole new rhythm to your life and perception
- backtrack to discover where a thought came from
- abstain from weight loss gimmicks
- let nature tutor you
- be able to forget
- buy from family farmers
- send a constructive personal opinion telegram to your senator
- invite friends over on a regular basis
- express how you feel concisely and clearly
- untangle something that was tangled

 instant karma

- let your hair dry in the sun
- conquer temptation
- inventory your daily life
- do exercises where you learn to see more by being actively prepared to see something
- in order to see, listen; in order to hear, look
- check out the class reading lists of a good college bookstore
- contemplate that all experiences, including life itself, do not arise by chance but through the coming together of all the necessary causes and conditions
- donate nice used china to a nursing home
- remember that an ending is a beginning in disguise
- call your friends, even if it's not your "turn"
- even when a situation is not in your control, your reaction to it is
- be kind to the child in you
- restrain yourself from acting on angry impulses

- campaign against the littering of outer space
- look things in the face and know them for what they are
- give a back scratch
- say a bedtime prayer
- don't exhaust yourself trying to avoid all disease
- make a bunch of peanut butter and jelly sandwiches to give to the local shelter
- take responsibility for your reactions
- on May Day, leave a basket at your sweetheart's front door
- wave to the elderly
- if you are living with another person, make an agreement that as soon as either of you starts to blame the other, you will end the argument
- keep a clean, well-organized kitchen, use well-washed ingredients, and set your table with pride
- keep what you learn in perspective

 instant karma

- the Buddha's words are pointers in the right direction, but you have to change your own heart and mind
- think of what you can do differently to start a positive cycle and improve a relationship
- let kindness, generosity, love, and wisdom motivate your intentions and happiness will follow
- surround yourself with pleasant aromas
- ask for the grace to realize who you are and the courage you will need to do so
- All I have seen teaches me to trust the Creator for all I have not seen (Ralph Waldo Emerson)
- accept responsibility
- when you feel yourself becoming impatient, remind yourself that the present situation will change
- send your mother-in-law flowers on your spouse's birthday
- forgive yourself for all the wrong things you have done and/or said

- miracles come after a lot of hard work
- learn Braille
- cultivate a restful home environment
- make an alphabet cereal message *I-L-O-V-E-Y-O-U* on toast or a plate
- wave hello to a pedestrian in the crosswalk
- compose a haiku in a restful place, preferably outside
- immerse yourself in each action you take
- make a list of favorite vegetarian foods and keep it handy
- start a patchwork quilt for someone
- learn to recognize the major forms of music and their subtypes
- leave sleepy people alone
- put money in someone's parking meter
- write a list of all the good things that have happened in your life
- be a shepherd — lead from behind

- plant a living Christmas tree each year
- see how desire arises and affects your life
- air out the quilts
- make a long winter weekend special for kids
- make Easter dinner for your in-laws
- take full advantage of the wondrous opportunities for growth and meaning
- increase yin with fruits (especially citrus), soft or watery vegetables, dairy products, frozen foods, refined oils
- be mindful of your own actions, not those of others
- appreciate small joys: showers, driving, singing, walking, freedom
- whenever you take, try to give back something
- identify one thing that you can change about your life today — no matter how small — and do it
- raise the subject of a disagreement without hostility
- get yourself into a state of "being" rather than "doing"

- buy your cat a scratching post
- do deep-breathing exercises to replenish your prana (energy)
- concentrate on health and light
- stop searching for happiness in someone else
- eat fresh fruit in season, supplementing with dried fruits
- if it is not dirty, do not wash it
- love can only exist in the present moment
- clear your life of flaky friends
- practice self-sufficiency, self-respect, and the discipline of hard work
- write your ideas down
- check your motivation
- mow an elderly neighbor's lawn
- make sure a fire is completely out
- type your child's first résumé
- read to someone who is cooking

- do your inner work every day
- see anger and desire as delusions that paint a false picture of reality
- avoid adopting others' negative views
- plan less
- prepare your Christmas card and gift list before Thanksgiving
- share holidays with your best friends
- slow your overall approach to life to a humane pace
- let go of resentment
- life is short; there is no time to waste
- wait without tapping your foot
- set up a family garage-cleaning session
- the next time you crave a material good, wait at least twenty-four hours before you give into it
- the first chakra is your root center, located at the base of the spine and associated with the color yellow; when it is in balance, you feel secure and brave

- read to a child every night before bed
- surround yourself with inspiration
- listen to your dreams
- add rose petals to your hot milk bath
- read about famous discoverers, creators, and inventors
- think of others when pursuing your own happiness
- put a cute note in your child's lunch box
- be an example of the value of hard work
- Be the change you want to see in the world (Mahatma Gandhi)
- un-learn fear, guilt, anger, jealousy, insecurity, and negativity
- go nonalcoholic
- offer apples and vegetables to birds and animals in winter
- Love truth, but pardon error (Voltaire)
- buy a back-saver snow shovel or a snowblower for the family member who clears the sidewalks

- go to a church and light a candle
- do your karmic homework
- make a happy snowman
- campaign to save the rain forests
- be an effective leader by seeking good ideas from all levels
- find and honor your own pace
- pack sunscreen for each kid
- use breathing as a kind of psychic first aid when events are too intense
- there is nothing to be, nothing to do, and nothing to have
- live for something other than "stuff"
- dress your bed in colorful sheets
- think before you act
- recognize that even the most exasperating person has Buddha nature within
- give yourself up to whatever the moment brings

- develop your own rituals of healing and repairing the world
- if you don't attach to the things that cause you stress, they can't cause you stress
- sing to your favorite music
- practice the Cobra Pose to open your heart chakra and strengthen your back
- keep in mind that you are connected to every other person on the planet
- sharpen your vision
- put your hand over your heart when you pledge allegiance
- slow down and enjoy what you have worked so hard for
- be a hero to someone
- only when you become empty can you be filled with something greater
- populate your to-do list, not your mind
- toast marshmallows

- put food in a bird feeder
- remind yourself that no matter what happens, this day will be over less than twenty-four hours from now
- choose not to waste your life on guilt about the past or concern for the future
- take the time to plump your dog's doggy bed
- thank someone for keeping your secret
- try not to use shopping as entertainment
- learn to be instead of do
- life is about loving and being loved
- refuse to be labeled
- offer to dog-sit when a friend goes away
- turn your home into a place of peace and simplicity
- relish the preparations for dinner
- visualize your goals
- by improving children's education, you improve the future of mankind
- have the confidence to imagine reaching your goals

- learn to recognize your own stress
- always keep pens and paper nearby
- when crabby, take an afternoon nap
- read to the driver on long trips
- share a soda fountain treat
- use thyme to help energize *kapha dosha*
- it's not what you do but why you do it
- buy a ticket to the opera
- go caroling with friends
- light up a room
- tailor learning to your life and interests
- take a retreat from the outside world
- pick a person at random and send them
  a greeting card
- only worry about yourself and your own actions
- hug someone even if they're mad
- ask more than usual of yourself
- round tables represent family harmony and equality

343 instant karma

- make a tape or CD for someone who shares your taste in music
- take adequate time for contemplation and reflection
- lying on your back, do the Stretch Pose — raise your head, hands, and heels six inches off the ground and begin the breath of fire; do this for one to three minutes for the third chakra
- embrace virtue
- you will be like those with whom you surround yourself
- notice how your hunger for possessions diminishes as you watch less TV and read fewer magazines
- prepack lunches to alleviate morning craziness
- tell yourself how warm you feel instead of thinking about how cold you are
- reuse packaging
- have no doubts
- there is peace in being nobody and having nothing
- schedule time for your inner work

- embrace people with acceptance and openness
- coexist gracefully with the unresolved
- let go of your attachment to the outcome
- to improve communication, clarify what you hear by paraphrasing
- when you are with kids, respect what they say and do
- accept your feelings, even the ones you wish you did not have
- send Thanksgiving cards
- wear bright colors on dark days
- stay centered in today because next week can take care of itself
- visualize your adversary performing an unexpected act of kindness
- enjoy freedom from want
- save the Great Barrier Reef
- observe your own mind and you will understand suffering and you will understand dharma

- enjoy a moment of thankful silence before you eat
- feast on crisp green salads
- consciously experience and appreciate life at home
- find the best baby-sitter for your kids
- don't underestimate the power of kindness
- find illustrative metaphors in nature
- be part of a husband-and-wife team
- get off mailing lists
- use fabric softener for the cotton sheets
- call your mother every Sunday
- think good thoughts
- get a crash-proof computer
- watch butterflies play tag
- Follow through on all your generous impulses (Epictetus)
- walk on a deserted beach and collect seashells
- what is the most important change you want for the world — and are you helping this change happen?

- refuse to agonize over what you can do nothing about
- associate and communicate well with others
- value silence and its eloquence
- give thanks
- stop rationalizing
- brush your cat or dog regularly
- if you can't fix it, call someone who can
- ban unconstructive criticism
- get excited about another person's idea
- feel your heart when you smile
- meditate on a beautiful painting
- save first, spend later
- never air dirty laundry
- it's all a game — so play well with others
- commit to what you can do
- keep going and continually begin again
- open the lines of communication
- bring a bag of doughnut holes to an officemate

 instant karma

- when something is worrying you, ask yourself if it is something you can control; if you can't control it, let it go
- take a nursing home resident out for a walk
- bring coffee to someone still in bed
- spritz your face with rosewater for a post-lunch pick-me-up
- pay no attention to things that do not concern you
- go to parades
- be willing to say "I don't know"
- wink
- finish every day and be done with it
- speak to your children with respect
- practice your yoga routine while the rest of the family is watching television
- be grateful for quiet times
- practice renunciation, a fundamental component of awakening

- stretch your mind and body in new directions
- learn to wait; once you can wait, you can do almost anything
- spend a day in the woods with nothing but your journal
- try the mantra: I am peace
- To thine own self be true (Shakespeare)
- hold babies, kittens, and puppies any chance you get
- let go of your need to broadcast
- whisper when appropriate
- take a deep breath and soften your response
- a successful life is one lived in friendship and love
- be in charge of what enters your mind
- take a walk when the world is too much
- clean up the garden at the end of September
- read *A Christmas Carol,* Charles Dickens's tale of karma
- encourage a child's interest in crossword puzzles
- You become what you think about all day long (Ralph Waldo Emerson)

- three essentials for happiness: something to do, something to hope for, someone to love
- lose a few pounds
- learn touch typing
- change what needs changing
- pass along copies of magazines to those who are sick or shut-in
- live sanely and gracefully, and without regret
- through constant contemplation, you can arrive at the truth
- make sure that everyone you know goes to vote
- share job-seeking strategies with those who need help
- dancing is a great way to get a workout and have fun
- consume less refined sugar
- when you travel, note people's similarities
- accept the beauty offered you for what it is
- be a cheering influence
- think you're a kid again

 instant karma 352

- experience your pain rather than try to distract yourself from it
- breathe while concentrating on the third eye
- sometimes the best use of your mind is not to use it at all
- appreciate your state of continual "becoming"
- kid around (lovingly) with a child
- lower your speed to lower your stress
- whoever listens most usually controls the situation
- understand that other people are going through difficulties, too
- get a cereal variety pack for kids having a sleepover
- take your in-laws to brunch after church
- memorialize someone at the Memorial Day party
- search out the positive
- gently heat a cup of low-fat milk, and add a tablespoon of honey and a pinch of dried ginger for a destressing drink

- never complain, never explain
- be ecstatic and filled with divine intoxication
- donate to the local animal shelter (blankets, cat litter, food, towels)
- practice deep breathing while running your bathwater or drying your hair
- just witnessing the dawn each day is a wake-up call
- take charge of your life
- read to your children
- walk a country lane on a cool morning
- include children in your conversations
- add one positive aspect to your life every week
- say prayers of thanksgiving
- choose wisely
- respect others' need for privacy
- in your spiritual life, the greatest changes are made slowly and gradually
- honesty brings peace

- change your head!
- truth-telling begins by becoming aware of what you tell yourself
- never forget who you are or where you came from
- express your positive feelings, no matter how trivial they seem
- take some time to be really silly
- visit a church library for some inspirational reading
- glow all day
- answer children's letters to Santa Claus
- even when you're angry, treat the other person with respect
- focus on the positive in your life, for what you focus on increases
- plant-sit for a friend
- learn all three yoga Warrior Poses to obtain inner peace
- show someone the ropes

- in a cross-legged position (Easy Pose), stretch your arms straight up and move them back and forth 6 to 9 inches for four minutes to balance the brain's hemispheres (the seventh chakra)
- along with a good-night kiss, tell your child you appreciate all the good things he or she did that day
- visit all the museums you can
- when cold, be thoroughly cold; when hot, be thoroughly hot — become one with the environment
- ask grandparents to tape bedtime stories for their grandchildren
- be good-natured
- keep your photograph albums up-to-date
- peace depends on the existence of love
- nothing can make your life more beautiful than perpetual kindness
- choose a response instead of being carried away by a reaction

- do the unexpected
- aerate your faucets to use less water
- work until you become tired, but not until you become exhausted
- if your irritation remains, step back and get a perspective on it
- listen to the pearls of wisdom that fall from other people's lips
- don't hog the overhead compartment on the airplane
- let your children see you do things for your spouse that show how much you treasure him or her
- honestly accept and acknowledge a wound
- do something mentally or physically rewarding
- turn off the TV and return to your self
- stretch before you go to sleep
- remember what you have learned
- lessen your food intake to lengthen your life
- give the gift of tenderness

 instant karma

- be open to constructive criticism, and learn even from hostile opinions
- smile at babies
- use thoughts and words of strength and love
- A man who wants to control his animal passions easily does so if he controls his palate (Mahatma Gandhi)
- take a kid to an Army-Navy store
- have a real, honest conversation with your parents
- shun evil
- at the end of the day, note five things you did for others and five things you did for yourself
- participate in a march for a good cause
- admire the virtues of others
- revel in time alone
- visit someone in a care facility
- We don't receive wisdom; we must discover it for ourselves after a journey that no one can take for us or spare us (Marcel Proust)

- once you lose the fear of dying, you truly begin to live
- take someone to work when their car is being repaired
- clear the clutter from each day
- take a dog for a walk in the country
- read the classics
- look into the eyes of loved ones when you are talking to them
- get to work on time
- value wholeness in your food
- participate in purposeful giving
- use common sense
- be hospitable
- look for something bright and beautiful in nature
- help enforce litter laws in your town
- tape a love note to the refrigerator
- have deep and calm feelings
- find out the source of a pain before taking anything for it

- use violet in the bedroom or area of meditation
- Enlightenment is intimacy with all things (Jack Kornfield)
- sponsor an elementary student through college
- adopt the attitude that the answer or resolution to a koan will come in time
- campaign against strip-mining
- conduct your activities consciously
- learn to say thank you in the language of every country you visit
- give a generous tip to a punctual or otherwise great taxi driver
- be the first to forgive
- continue what you have begun
- partake in the tea ceremony, which symbolizes respect for others, harmony, sincerity, and tranquility of the soul
- study Hindu and Buddhist dharma

- help preserve sand dunes
- watch the kids play at the beach
- every day you have an opportunity to learn
- be a person who says positive things about others
- learn the art of detachment
- never cut what can be untied
- the little things in life are as interesting as the big ones
- have a capacity as vast as the ocean and a mind as open as space
- work as a team with your partner and family
- do not resist a nap if it has been a tiring day
- write a "You're Welcome" card in reply to a "Thank You" card
- play a brain-stimulating card game, like bridge, to boost your immune system
- if you think you owe an apology, an explanation, or money, you probably do
- tao is flowing, just like a river

- each day, pause to do layered listening — the loudest, obvious sounds and then the next layer down, etc.
- pace yourself
- try a meditation for breaking habits: sit cross-legged with thumbs firmly pressing your temples, lock the molars together and release (like biting down) for 5 to 7 minutes
- consider the amount of time desire causes us to waste
- ask, "At the end of my life, how much will it really mean to me to fulfill this desire?"
- sample Hosshin koans, which give insight into emptiness, the essence of all things
- order the mind, replenish the heart
- consciously choose to think of people to love
- fix squeaking doors that could wake people
- stop every few minutes while eating and check how full you feel
- turn off TV, turn on life

- Do no harm, act for the good, purify the mind (Buddha)
- learn the language of the country you are visiting
- sit down and really think out an attitude of yours that you're not sure of
- go with the flow of things
- set your loved ones free — then they will be free to love you
- combine warmth with understanding
- drink aromatic tea with breakfast
- be specific and direct about what you want to communicate
- rummage for finds at a flea market
- wrap up a favorite article of clothing that someone always borrows and give it to them
- drop assumptions
- consider giving a teenager a form of communication — a pager, a cell phone, etc.

- sample Nanto koans, which point to a subtle place beyond all opposites and lead to tranquility
- stop using disposable cups
- be kind to yourself when you let yourself down
- savor freedom
- write things down; your mind can hold only about seven chunks of information at a time
- do twenty-six figure-eight neck rolls for your fifth chakra
- start the day with peppermint tea
- fill half the stomach with food, one-quarter with liquid, and leave the rest empty
- share your strength
- climb a tree to do some constructive daydreaming
- find a main form of entertainment that is not TV
- wear a favorite cologne every day
- think of time spent waiting as free time
- when there is deceit, offer the truth

- welcome those moments when you can take a deep breath and gather yourself before proceeding anew
- know your sport: its requirements, risks, benefits, preparations
- use your fireplace
- volunteer in a political campaign
- lead a blameless life
- be like the mountain in the face of a strong wind, firm and steady
- make special comforting foods for someone who is sick
- overlook no opportunity to play and laugh
- rush home for Thanksgiving
- admit your mistakes
- give your dad a tape of old-time radio shows
- act the part and you will become the part
- walk in a stately manner
- stop, sit, breathe, listen, look, feel, smell
- ask what action you can take to get yourself to your goal

 instant karma

- support organic farming
- invite friends to share a celebration
- leave behind the day-to-day business of your life while you are cooking
- look into *Marma* puncture, the Ayurvedic equivalent of acupuncture
- find at least one thing that you can let go each day
- don't just walk away from negative people: run!
- give steaming cups of Earl Grey tea to winter hikers
- cultivate virtue by what you read, listen to, and watch
- conduct every transaction with fairness and honor
- be here now
- immerse yourself in a subject you are interested in
- donate a computer to a school
- learn to be by yourself
- be motivated by compassion and the Way
- try biofeedback
- go confidently in the direction of your dreams

- ask yourself daily how you can cut down on the paper products you use
- send a postcard to your grandparents
- try to be amused by things you once took seriously — someone cutting in front of you, for example
- rejoice in your spouse's graces
- save yourself rather than attempt to save humanity
- take responsibility for your part in your relationships
- organize, but only after you have simplified
- swim more rivers
- provide a character role model
- practice yoga while waiting for the laundry to dry
- take the time to look through old photo albums
- forget yesterday and forget tomorrow; you can't have yesterday back and tomorrow never really comes
- take a course at an arts-and-crafts center
- believe that you will recover from a setback
- be open to life

- leave coins in someone's garden
- spend as much time as you can
  pursuing pleasurable activities
- remove words like "can't" from your mental vocabulary
- start your day by reading the comics
- stand under a waterfall
- share
- give extra kisses
- be your mate's electric blanket
- read books on Zen and the Tao
- Buddhism's Right Understanding is recognizing
  the unity of all beings
- concentrate on the everyday routine
- drop your act in front of others
- overcome fear
- use green, a lucky color in feng shui, to soothe
  the energy of your home
- realize that something special is often very simple

- deliver fresh flowers regularly to the local nursing home
- be as polite to your children as you want them to be to you
- make sure there are clean, dry towels in the bathrooms
- resist the temptation to judge and talk about others
- help your child produce a "Me" book with photos, friends, hobbies, etc.
- give away tickets you can't use
- have eyes only for your partner
- the spaces between our words are often more profound than the chatter
- keep your mouth sweet and clean
- let go of superstitions
- make your own baby food
- sit in a library and smell the books
- keep your pet on a leash

- remind yourself to be patient
- go on a spiritual retreat
- put money in its place
- buy what you need and buy what you love
- plan your meals as if each were a still life painting
- exchange pet- and house-sitting with neighbors
- write poetry for yourself or others
- visualize your future
- have an abundance of houseplants for absorbing carbon dioxide
- let it be
- eat at regular intervals
- attend the opening night of a performance
- explore new places, stay curious
- feel joy before the gift is given and give gracefully
- avoid hot, oily foods in summer
- while meditating, focus on one of the chakras, such as the one between the eyebrows or the one at the heart

- eat at home more often
- challenge your assumptions
- take your dog for a swim on a hot summer day
- know what to do when your body gets the blues
- throw an anniversary party for your parents
- begin to eliminate your need for perfection
- find another use for something that is currently unused
- donate your books to churches, hospitals, halfway houses, or prisons
- wait for weight loss
- when you eat, just eat
- look for opportunities to validate others
- be thankful for someone who has been generous in spirit
- Work is love made visible (Kahlil Gibran)
- karma means you don't get away with anything
- give meaningful holiday gifts

- do all you can to create harmony
- win the respect of intelligent persons
- be aware of the snowball effect of your thinking
- be gentle, be kind, be thoughtful, be caring, be compassionate, be fair, be generous
- help children think for themselves
- before you get out of bed each morning, take five minutes to listen, see, smell, breathe, observe
- celebrate each new day with a good deed
- take it for granted that things will go wrong
- to live a creative life, you must lose the fear of being wrong
- never hurry
- imagine living your life without judging others
- always be there for your family
- make a list of your good qualities
- strengthen your skills
- schedule lunch with an encouraging friend

- greet family with a kiss and a hug
- invest in some funny audio tapes for a friend who is sick
- carry your loved ones' pictures in your wallet
- resist messages that constantly urge you to eat, eat, eat
- say "NO" to fur
- live life as if the time left to you is a pleasant surprise
- prioritize rather than become overwhelmed with all your to-dos
- quietly close doors
- encourage anyone who is trying to improve
- set flexible goals for yourself
- expect that you will make good choices
- at least once a day, sit and do nothing
- when the time is right, teach your kids about the birds and bees
- learn the rules of mind mapping, intended to help your judgment and understanding

- have without possessing
- participate in holistic health care
- when you do a good deed, be grateful that you had the chance to do it
- improve your flexibility
- lose yourself in a child's world
- bake a birthday cake
- to see others' joy as your own, learn the way of nonattachment
- get in the spiritual flow
- learn to show cheerfulness, even when you don't feel it
- get to know your children's friends
- relax and realign by lying semi-supine, with your head propped up an inch or two
- carry a portable talisman
- consult an expert when it is called for
- to take care of the planet is to take care of your own house

- study the spiritual traditions of the world to deepen your understanding
- send an e-mail or leave a voice-mail message just to say, "I love you"
- have a sense of humor about your age
- know that you can handle anything
- breathe fully and completely to gain mental clarity and physical endurance
- let others explain their side of a story
- stop periodically and bring yourself back to the present
- look at unpleasant feelings and realize they will pass
- cleanse your mind of all the clutter, the stuff that does you no good
- resist the temptation to brag
- total absorption in the task is zazen
- a good parent is one who helps the child care for and take care of himself
- let the dharma teach you and it will become your truth

- design and help build a children's playground
- offer feelings of security
- read *1001 Ways to Be Romantic*
- brush someone else's hair
- slow down
- say thank you consciously and from the heart
- find a way to see each source of discontentment in some positive light
- correct transgressions, don't dwell on them
- when you are feeling out of control and resentful toward all you have to do, the best strategy is to relax and breathe
- give the gift of a personal trainer for a new mom
- get an extra hour of sleep when you need it
- learn new synonyms for words you use a lot
- find your very best self
- attachment to "how life should be" is the greatest impediment to the spiritual path

- plan physical feats to celebrate milestone birthdays
- stop trying to do it all
- when you have a cup of coffee, live the moment
- sell a too-expensive house
- make sure your feet are warm for sleeping
- appreciate a Technicolor sunset
- ask yourself, "What is this other person trying to teach me?"
- fix something without being asked
- be the pause that refreshes
- practice listening for the spaces between sounds
- thrive on inner peace
- work together
- steal a few minutes alone in the morning to sit with your private plans, thoughts, feelings
- don't push yourself beyond the comfort zone
- refuse to quit learning
- be thankful for plants

- warm someone's socks
- revive tired furniture
- mean what you say
- invite friends to sample a new recipe
- help find homes for stray pets
- take time to reevaluate your goals on a regular basis
- look for clues from within
- as a meditation, listen to sound with focused awareness
- let go of fear
- toss guilt up in the air and let the wind carry it away
- meditation and active spiritual efforts bring dynamic development
- identify more with the inner part of yourself — the part that doesn't grow older
- consciously let go of tension or compulsiveness
- acknowledge the good things about your partner
- make "family time" each day
- take pictures of your children's "big" events

- be both strong and caring
- sketch the beauty around you
- use feng shui items such as mirrors and crystals for harmonious flow of *chi*
- acknowledge a child's wounds, no matter how slight
- master a magic trick for kids
- read a Girl Scout or Boy Scout handbook
- listen with compassion
- at the end of each day, let your thoughts idle for a while
- use lavender to help soothe you to sleep
- cook gourmet recipes rather than spend money at a restaurant
- give yourself permission to do nothing
- look up definitions
- be good-hearted
- live in such a way that your behavior causes no embarrassment
- never hate, never resist, never contest

- surprise a loved one with a box of chocolates
- write thank-you notes promptly
- read a dictionary in your field of work or your strongest area of interest
- suppress your inner critic
- draw on everything you know
- release bitterness
- buy an avid reader an embosser that stamps in books "The Library of [Name]"
- massage someone's scalp
- be sensitive to other people's boundaries
- write something at the end of every day
- help a neighbor put up their Christmas lights
- volunteer at the library
- accept situations without trying to change them
- work/serve/contribute
- donate money to your alma mater
- relax without the use of chemical substances

- leave work at work and home life at home
- enjoy being calm when others around you are not
- nourish your guests mentally, physically, spiritually
- a mantra can help you feel more energized
- one thing completed is worth ten things on hold
- support politicians working for affordable health care and insurance
- use your intuition to see whether what you want is based in love or fear
- take classes in healthy cooking
- make a sense of humor your greatest asset
- give "red-carpet" welcomes
- apologize even if you don't think you were wrong
- compel curiosity in others
- stop the busy work
- the more you think of others, the happier you are
- liberate your husband from a traditional male task now and then

- **think the most interesting thoughts**
- exercise your taste buds: eat something sour, pungent, or spicy
- imagine yourself free of aches, pains, illness, and tension
- serve dinner with artistry
- never stop adapting
- drink your tea slowly
- close your eyes to the faults of others
- take time to breathe, absorb, assess
- stop going back to the same people for the same rejections
- always think twice
- live your life as if the most secret corners of your soul were open to the sight of others
- sample Goi koans, which are difficult, but lead to final insight into the apparent and the real
- the way to keep young is to keep your faith young

- join a political group that is reasonable, thoughtful, and purposeful
- what is needed is less: less greed, less fear, less hatred, less prejudice
- love to listen
- perform the unexpected
- accepting things as they are is the foundation of great strength
- periodically go through your drawers, cabinets, and bookshelves and get rid of things you no longer need
- start a standing ovation
- practice nonviolence
- wallpaper a room for your mom
- make people laugh
- applaud even the smallest of successes
- feed animals natural food
- use the mantra *om shanti shanti shanti* to balance and bring peace to body, mind, and spirit

- be in love with the world
- stop thinking about how you wish it could be and realize how good you've got it
- throw away three-quarters of the papers in your files
- use campfire chants as a mantra
- regularly phone or visit your oldest relative
- Every time a thought arises, throw it away . . . the thoughts are like clouds — when the clouds have cleared, the moon appears (Daito)
- recognize your coworkers' contributions
- show a traveler his way
- take the first step with a good thought, the second with a good word, the third with a good deed
- what might you release that would lighten you?
- know that at each moment, you are creating something for the future
- teach children to take a moment alone whenever they need it

- live magnanimously
- buoy yourself by proving your capability
- support your local parades
- listen to Tchaikovsky's lilting *Nutcracker Suite*
- hang a pleasant-sounding wind chime in front of your home or office
- always accept an outstretched hand
- offer assistance if you see a neighbor having a problem
- be grateful for the gift of every day
- enjoy the fresh, clear quietness of a country morning
- Genius is infinite patience (Michelangelo)
- walk tall
- be determined to live a happy life
- study hard, whatever the subject
- practice mindfulness in the kitchen
- leave a food treat in the pantry for someone to discover
- bag your garbage nicely for the garbage collector
- laugh with others

- floss
- open your home to someone in need
- trust yourself to get through a difficult time
- for peace of mind, your bed should face the door
- sit down to meditate with no thought of results or gain
- give your thought a specific direction
- before bed, write down three things that can help you
  solve a problem
- be someone's knight in shining armor
- send out goodness and you can expect goodness
  to come back to you
- appreciate all the help you get along the way
- ban all media input from your life (television, radio,
  newspaper) to help clear your karma
- regularly replace your toothbrush
- play footsie
- merge courteously
- withhold criticism or judgment

- plant tulip bulbs or daffodils for a nursing home
- wear a wildflower in your lapel
- support the local schools
- throw a cast party after the school play
- spend fifteen minutes a day learning a foreign language you have always wanted to learn
- make few promises
- limit yourself to thinking about one subject as you go to sleep
- make someone smile
- use blue in bedrooms to ensure a good night's rest
- live without television
- send endearing letters
- take part in mindful commuting
- make your life more like you want it
- put together an emergency-preparedness kit
- welcome friends who drop in
- weed and groom the garden

- keep your front entrance and passageways completely clear
- calm your mind with three deep breaths
- thank your customers
- protect life that is weaker than you are
- shake hands with enthusiasm
- buy your partner a bathrobe or nightshirt
- share knowledge freely
- make your sweetheart's favorite meal
- avoid using insecticides
- put out the welcome mat
- pay attention, be relaxed, enjoy what you do
- be willing to act in the face of fear
- tap your awareness of what you already know
- put effort into your life
- invite an elderly person to dinner or a movie
- know how precious and sweet life is
- ask productive questions

- Zen means that if you want to understand what a watermelon is, you take a watermelon, get a knife, cut the watermelon, and put a slice in your mouth — it is your experience
- be easy to get along with
- make a difference in the life of someone you care about
- have a reputation for spunk
- cheer at your children's sporting events
- eat around the same times every day
- draw out the best in others by being an example yourself
- seize every opportunity
- begin your practice of generosity with giving away material things
- make a breakfast tray for someone, complete with bud vase and crossword puzzle
- look after the sick as you would look after yourself

- remember who you knew you were when you were a child
- give money to the bride and groom, even if you gave a present
- Practice not-doing and everything will fall into place (Lao-tzu)
- smell the green grass
- kindness calms the mind
- kick up your heels
- at least once a day, tell your partner how terrific he is and that you love him
- our home, children, and body are given to us for a short while — treat them with care and respect
- repair a lamp yourself, with the help of a do-it-yourself book
- hold doors for others
- find consolation in all things
- make amends to those you've harmed

- be easy to speak to, gentle and not proud
- substitute flexibility for rigidity
- monitor your intake of sugar, salt, caffeine, and alcohol
- exercise early in the day to raise your metabolism
- the more creative you are, the more fun your children will have
- be able to say, "I made it myself"
- study philosophy
- garden inside if you have no choice, but garden!
- let go of your need to be overly involved
- hold someone tenderly when she is crying
- wake up New Year's Day knowing you didn't make a fool of yourself the night before
- if you are congested, spray a little eucalyptus essential oil around your pillow
- cultivate the seven virtues: charity, faith, fortitude, hope, justice, prudence, temperance
- send a thank-you note to your child's teacher

- wash your hands and face with cold water to neutralize or discharge yang *chi*
- help Grandma blow out her birthday candles
- give more than you planned to give
- the Zen approach to worry is simple: just don't
- be a good loser and a good winner
- don't fill your body with rubbish food
- feed a hummingbird
- hire well-trained baby-sitters
- find happiness with what you have and with who you are
- use environmentally friendly dishwasher detergent
- don't take anything personally
- learn from your misery and pain
- undertake challenging activities instead of easy ones
- eat foods that are rich in iron, such as fortified cereals, tofu, whole grains, and legumes
- commit yourself to doing what is possible

- Happiness is never stopping to think if you are (Paul Sondreal)
- there are no mistakes in life, only lessons
- pay attention to your impulses
- give up trying to be right
- have love and loyalty for your country
- What is essential is invisible to the eye (Antoine de St. Exupéry)
- meet deadlines
- a neat, clean environment is conducive to good living and clear thinking
- act brave until you really feel brave
- wear colorful workout clothing for positive feng shui
- work on trusting people
- fill your mind with healthy thoughts
- be awake to interconnections
- clear out files seasonally
- like all of your mate's friends

393 instant karma

- a loving act bears loving fruit
- worthy actions can bring many benefits
- practice doing work that has no reward
- don't overreact to life's bumps
- say a centering prayer
- don't try to convince others
- consider that your suffering comes from your attitude and not from experiences themselves
- don't be disturbed by trifles or by common or unavoidable accidents
- make a list of the places you want to go and make a hobby of vacation-planning
- support international food organizations
- Learn to labor and to wait
  (Henry Wadsworth Longfellow)
- give generously to things that will last beyond your lifetime
- see what happens if you simply watch and listen

- do not criticize
- get up earlier and walk to work
- become an eternal optimist
- be active in at least one community organization
- practice letting go of disappointment
- give a thing your wholehearted attention
- strengthen family togetherness
- remember more isn't always better
- be an advocate for human rights
- send an unsigned card or valentine to the person you have a crush on
- read your computer manual
- give children toys that are powered by imagination
- walk barefoot on the grass
- celebrate new beginnings with a vegetarian barbecue
- don't hurry — each second, each minute of life is a miracle
- have faith in yoga

- slot in a time for exercise
- get rid of attitudes that have reinforced your possessive aspects
- make a direct donation to a homeless person
- try to have a consistent bedtime and waking time
- invite your mom to lunch
- praise every improvement
- clean under the rugs
- help someone out who has just had cataract surgery
- spend a lot of time with your kids
- sit outside and look at the moon and stars
- gain energy by exerting energy
- develop your greatest talent further
- set a plate filled with food in front of a hungry teenager
- play Santa Claus at a Christmas party
- go on an Audubon Society vacation
- give yourself time to adapt to change

- activity is contagious
- surrender your weight issues to a Higher Power
- give your child accurate feedback, grounding him or her in reality
- use what's at hand to simplify your life and home
- when facing a difficult task, act as though it is impossible to fail
- start a fire in the fireplace on a rainy summer evening
- discard all jealousy
- help a child to write and illustrate his or her own book
- think of all sounds as being the Buddha's voice — the barking dog, the loud party next door
- clear the table after a meal
- brush your teeth mindfully
- protect your children from stress if possible
- keep the same baby-sitter for years
- use natural, not chemical, air fresheners
- volunteer to cuddle premature infants

- meditate on the quality you would like to have more of in your life
- communicate your respect for your child's ability to learn
- fix someone a favorite meal at an unexpected time
- Be islands unto yourselves; be refuges unto yourselves; hold fast to the dharma as an island; hold fast to the dharma as a refuge; seek not for refuge in anyone except yourselves. (Buddha)
- everything happens for a good reason
- populate your environment with objects of sentimental or aesthetic appeal
- say you are sorry and mean it
- it is okay for you to feel okay
- put crumbs out for winter animals
- step back from your own mind in order to understand all things
- believe tolerance is a virtue

- "smoke" chocolate cigarettes
- touch another person with presence and caring
- act with integrity
- when you are tempted to use words as weapons,
  ask yourself what you hope to gain
- doodle
- eat foods that are rich in vitamin C
- make sure all the house flashlights are operational
- try coupling an awareness of walking with
  an awareness of breathing
- take a class
- allow others to be right; stop correcting
- make hard decisions with a soft heart
- learn the ropes
- enjoy the thought of reincarnation
- attune yourself to subtle changes in a speaker's tone,
  volume, and inflection
- return forgiveness and tolerance

399 instant karma

- give someone a lift when she takes her car in for service
- whichever seeds you water will blossom and grow into plants
- eat something green
- come home early from work to give your spouse a break from the kids
- compliment the parent of a well-behaved child
- run out after dinner for ice cream with the kids
- select an inspirational book to always have on hand to give to friends
- brush your teeth right after a meal
- be fully present for children during a special event or vacation
- acknowledge all the good things
- use, but don't abuse, others' talents
- love
- act with no expectations

- remain courteous in a crowded checkout line
- discover your destination — then take the easiest route
- write notes thanking people for what you have learned from them
- watch an army of ants work
- when you cook, do it because you love to cook
- act with a pure mind and happiness will follow you
- be a do-gooder
- facilitate the growth of others
- respect someone's silent thoughts
- put things back where they belong
- keep a supply of stickers to give to kids
- let go of the urge to fix someone else
- understand the spiritual side of simple living
- enrich your time with friends by being attentive, open, loving
- hang three coins on a red cord or string just inside the main door of a home to keep prosperity inside

 instant karma

- give a gift anonymously
- talk yourself through your anger
- be adequately prepared
- if you practice only one yoga pose, practice *shavasana* (Corpse Pose)
- learn to learn
- exercise your soul
- act with enthusiasm
- judge your actions by the value they create
- use less stuff
- calming your mind, you begin to calm your world
- send someone an article you know will be of special interest
- the Tao is always present within you, and you can use it any way you want
- take up weekend bicycling
- admire others' intelligence
- be ready for surprises around the corner

- the only thing you take with you is your karmic bank account
- master your appetites
- give someone the weather forecast if they are traveling the next day
- let your stomach tell you when to stop eating
- have the heart of a child
- wear a bright-colored raincoat
- always keep the door ajar
- try progressive relaxation: tightening and then loosening various muscles
- laugh at someone's favorite story — again
- enjoy campfire camaraderie
- visualize your goals just before you go to sleep
- carry spares
- barter or swap
- take time to be playful today
- notice the world outside your window

- perform a 5- to 10-minute, all-over scalp and body massage first thing in the morning with an oil like jojoba or sesame
- train your mind to be in a good mood
- your three greatest treasures are simplicity, patience, compassion
- be inclusive and accepting, not judgmental and critical
- say a prayer of reconciliation
- give a sack of rice as a house-warming gift — it represents survival, prosperity, sustenance
- become a master of words
- make big batches of foods you love and freeze extra servings for later
- forgive and forget
- respect military personnel
- fight for academic freedom
- get plenty of sleep
- read good literature daily

- you are the only person who can "make" yourself feel anything
- greet your grandparents at the airport
- be grateful to those people who have made life most difficult for you
- find one hour a day to read, reflect, create
- help out with projects in the house and garden
- be willing to receive love without struggle
- roll down and relax into a rag doll, straighten your legs, breathe, then roll up
- stay out of the rat race
- have a loving relationship with your children
- don't buy something just because it's cheap
- take your brown-bag lunch to a scenic spot
- divide your to-do lists into A=vital, B=necessary, and C=trivial
- let someone else take the stage
- practice generosity of spirit

- love people and lead them without imposing your will
- make time to relax
- insist on quality
- Ask not what your country can do for you; ask what you can do for your country (John F. Kennedy)
- lessen your demands of others
- all of your happiness and all of your suffering are created by your own mind
- give thoughtful graduation gifts
- do your job with quiet competence
- live with passion
- give a pet the companionship it needs
- pay for a needy child to go to summer camp
- don't wait for someone else to make decisions for you
- air out a bedroom or house for an hour after burning incense
- seek out unusual taste experiences
- resist telling people how something should be done

- don't let any one activity dominate your day and you will cultivate an inner equilibrium and contentment
- be a camp counselor
- try palming; cupping your palms over your eyes two to three times a day for fifteen minutes to enhance your vision
- tend those who are sick in body or at heart
- take a kid to the library
- enjoy the art of tasting
- give thought-provoking books
- let go and let God
- accept praise and believe it as fast as you believe a criticism
- clean your desk before you go home for the day
- let the other person do a great deal of the talking
- use the earphones for your stereo
- understand your rhythms
- fill your plate with more vegetables and less meat

- take a long bicycle trip
- develop a mind that clings to nothing
- stop bemoaning how bad things are
- keep a journal you love
- drag yourself out of your sloth
- never trouble another for what you can do yourself
- spend your energy even more carefully than you spend your money
- appreciate the calm periods and make them last longer
- laugh until your cheeks hurt
- honor the specialness of family times spent together
- practice your child's sport with him or her
- live intentionally
- make your own valentines
- tiptoe around anyone who is sleeping
- live your ideals
- handle interruptions

- quit a bad job
- work for Amnesty International
- sit on a porch swing
- start a clothing drive for homeless people in your community
- with each weed you pull up, you make room for fresh green grass
- turn a meal into a feast
- take the road less traveled
- feeling angry is not wrong, but expressing anger in unproductive or hurtful ways is
- go the extra mile
- love many things
- create a "Welcome Home" banner as a surprise after the first day of school
- make the most of an educational opportunity
- try a breathing or walking meditation where a breath or step is "just" and the next one is "this"

- experience the Zen of housecleaning
- if you borrow someone's car, return it with a full tank of gas
- remember that anything can happen at anytime
- attend city council/selectman meetings, board of education meetings, or meetings of any other group that interests you
- give Mom and Dad a session with a photographer
- apply the techniques of walking meditation to your routine daily activities
- no matter how problematic the people in your life are, you are always the solution
- trim the fat from your diet
- gently remove an insect from your home
- consider those who point out your faults as your most benevolent teachers
- never stop trying to improve yourself
- share thoughts and ideas

- reach for the sky
- take in free kittens
- improve your attention and memory with notetaking
- You cannot travel on the path before you have become the Path itself (Buddha)
- participate actively in the P.T.A.
- keep up the family traditions
- create your own unique life
- explore different routes on your walks or runs
- according to feng shui, blue, green, or turquoise candles enhance knowledge, scholarly success, wisdom, experience, and self-development
- make sacrifices for the good of the family
- buy yourself one exotic bloom
- go to a late movie on a night when you will be able to sleep in
- cross something that you dreaded off a to-do list
- take a correspondence or distance-learning course

- be the first to say hello or give a kiss
- set up a touch football game for Thanksgiving, pre-turkey
- clean up after a great meal that someone prepared for you
- develop many interests outside of work
- strive for perfect attendance
- pay attention to how different kinds of music affect you
- meditate to get your mind in the right mode for the day
- believe that life is worth living
- live your life for others — seek and find how to serve
- get a personalized travel mug for a commuting friend
- help a child master the art of shoe-tying
- everything matters
- let every guest hang an ornament on your Christmas tree

- finish your work so you get the holiday off
- if you don't have time for a long workout, try two shorter ones
- become a less aggressive driver
- embrace solitude
- appreciate the cook by eating everything you are given
- call an older person regularly
- learn to love beans and nuts
- eliminate *must*, *ought*, and *should* from your vocabulary
- in calm moments, focus on creative problem-solving
- start a local historical society
- remain unperturbed by the unavoidable
- put mittens in a basket by the back door
- choose being happy over being right
- buy a pair of funny glasses for each member of your family
- help to create a nonviolent world
- notice happy sounds

- pass on some good news — but don't pass on gossip
- relinquish and renounce cravings
- appreciate the gleaming symmetry of a frosted spider web at dawn
- karma means watching your body, watching your mouth, and watching your mind
- expose your children to interesting things
- give a child responsibility
- give a compliment to a stranger
- if you want to be given everything, give everything up
- join a book club
- stop viewing time as the enemy
- we can all do much more than we think, but first we have to believe it
- sleep in decent nightclothes instead of old T-shirts
- try to make yourself laugh even when you see little to laugh about
- choose inner joy, not power

- developing your nature and embracing virtue is embodying the Tao
- invite someone to spend the weekend with you as a houseguest
- change the world one mind at a time
- do more than your share of work
- listen with a sense of humility
- look for ways to help nature
- laugh at life
- fight hunger
- toss the mail from solicitors unopened
- pick a nickname for your child that will enhance his or her self-image
- there is nothing to hold your negative feelings in place other than your own thinking
- it is as important to have formal meditation practice each day as it is to eat
- participate in taste tests and wine tastings

- take a two-mile walk after lunch
- notice the impression your life and deeds make upon other people
- put a first-aid kit in your driving-age child's car
- say hello every time you see a neighbor
- bear all cheerfully, do all bravely
- assign the kids some regular chores around the house
- Think only what is right there, what is right under your nose to do. It's such a simple thing — that's why people can't do it. (Henry Miller)
- take time to watch the sunset or sunrise
- fluff a child's pillow before they go to bed
- dance a little bit every day
- contemplate the way in which life depends on variety
- offer the window seat to the other passenger
- accept your experiences, even the ones you hate
- reflect on the inevitable impermanence of relationships

- learn the lessons that life presents
- free yourself from fear
- put things in perspective by reading "Today in History" snippets
- raja yoga is the yoga of meditation, merging the self with the universe
- give a friend a Top Ten list of reasons why they are great
- sit on the floor in a lotus position
- put a flower on someone's windshield
- invent new reasons to celebrate
- keep your bedroom free of clutter and with minimal furniture so that *chi* can flow easily through the room
- return borrowed items undamaged
- do the yoga chest expansion to stretch the shoulders and upper arms
- take your children to parades and parks
- make appointments with beginning and ending times

- fulfill a snack attack with a smoothie, fresh fruit, soy yogurt, popcorn, raw nuts, or fresh veggies
- adopt new ways of thinking
- notice the texture of the food you eat
- have lively discussions at dinner, but no arguments
- always keep a pair of dirty sneakers available
- rent a vacation getaway, beach house, or cabin and invite others to celebrate with you
- enjoy early mornings
- make children's snacks with creativity
- turn yourself inside out and discover the universe within
- become aware of your anger as soon as possible
- say hello to animals
- live for the moment
- participate in welcoming committees
- forget the symbols of success
- take an art appreciation course at a museum

- have friends who work as hard as you do
- help someone change a tire
- meditate in your own way
- paint a room with a color you have always liked
- do something out of the ordinary tonight
- drive with the radio turned off
- consume all good things in moderation
- let your mind free-associate, using the sounds and smells you experience
- if you know someone who is going through a difficult time, do something — anything — to let the person know you care
- work off excess energy from pent-up tension
- turn fear into adventure
- arise when the alarm goes off
- use a cell phone with discrimination and politeness
- sing all the hymns in church
- nothing is half as important as you usually think it is

- make sure your friends know you accept them as they are
- split a milkshake with your child
- offer to help a neighbor do a home improvement project, like painting
- make Kool-Aid for hot summer days
- feel heady with optimism and warmth
- when you are feeling most vulnerable, stick with the familiar
- play patty-cake with a baby
- appreciate and nurture potential
- bring home a surprise from a bake shop
- welcome the neighbors to an open house in your new home
- remember how passionately you yearned in the past for many of the things you do not like now
- rent your favorite videos
- be a wonderful weekend guest

- as you walk, think about walking and notice how it feels for your body to be moving
- be courageous enough to be open and receptive to different possibilities
- see to it that your home is a safe haven
- seeing the truth will never harm you — it will only free you
- have a weekly family-fun night
- say a holiday prayer
- try writing down your everyday hunches and intuitions
- give red-carpet treatment
- don't let discussions turn into arguments
- slow down and see where you are going
- toss a football around with a kid
- remember to look up and appreciate the sky
- act frankly
- volunteer as a tutor in the public schools
- look for bargains, but don't be cheap

- create beauty
- note the happy reactions of people
- express gratitude for life's riches on a regular basis
- throw yourself into your hobbies
- meet someone at the airport
- remember happiness can only be found within
- take it easy on yourself when you cannot make something happen
- learn to make peace with whatever is present
- invite a brother- or sister-in-law's kids to a sporting event
- balance your diet, with good amounts of protein and essential fatty acids, and a modest amount of carbohydrates
- play an active role in your child's education
- prefer smaller-scale living and working environments
- save your questions until the end of a lecture
- make a list of to-dos that are not time-sensitive

- be a student of life, always learning
- buy Girl Scout cookies and donate them to an organization
- let your children know that no matter what happens, you will always be there for them
- in moments of nongrasping, you can assess what is truly of value in your life
- do the very best you know how, the very best you can
- make peace with your past and with other people
- breathe and relax the heart
- accept that breaking a bad habit is a process
- feng shui is about becoming aware of your environment and applying energetic principles to your surroundings
- try to experience everything as though it were brand-new
- stop shopping with money you don't have
- let the chips fall where they may

- accept the fact that as you change, your relationships will change
- be sensitive to the person next to you
- notice beauty you might have overlooked before
- try eye compresses of zucchini soaked in chamomile or ginseng tea
- leave old habits and negativities behind
- you don't have all the time in the world, so don't waste it
- donate your used stuff
- move your computer out of your bedroom
- pay attention when someone has a problem
- take long vacations
- find a way to save something from every paycheck
- notice things
- respond to rudeness with kindness
- ask, "Am I awake? Where is my mind right now?"
- judge a tree by its fruits

- take advantage of opportunities to expand your friendship base
- work to keep your relationships vibrant
- a bowl of fruit offers continuous sustenance for you and your family
- imagine yourself building a snowman — off-load all your stress to him — then imagine the sun melting the snowman along with all your resentments
- take time to share your individual values, visions, and goals with your mate
- visit friends when they are in the hospital
- try not to allow yourself to be rushed, impatient, or anxious
- stick with something
- serve summer dinner out in the garden
- you can allow yourself to be vulnerable because you are strong
- let your intelligence be guided by positive motivation

 instant karma

- Zen demands attention to life's ordinary details — where we put things down, how we pick them up
- support manufacturing with a minimum of waste and pollution
- light a dark corner
- remember that your decisions affect other people
- do something that is "against all odds"
- the next time you feel inexplicably irritable or angry, stop and think about what is really bothering you
- align your thoughts and emotions with your intentions
- spend your bonus on a needy child
- a project or chore you don't want to do is exactly what you make of it: something interesting or a pain — your choice
- leave a surprise flower basket at someone's front door
- call when you're going to be late
- stop an argument in your mind before opening your mouth

- share your faith
- pay attention to the way you interact with your surroundings
- yield
- adopt a neglected garden
- make sure your will is in order and up-to-date
- each time you bring your wandering mind back during meditation, you weaken the compulsive cycle and strengthen mindfulness
- regain your sense of humor by making a funny face at yourself
- remember your anniversary
- pare down the possessions that rob you of energy
- learn to recognize desires but not be controlled by them
- note how much concentration it takes to follow every word of a verbal exchange
- make something for someone else

427 instant karma

- what a person takes in by contemplation, he pours out in love
- find your cure for writer's block
- write down every compliment or thanks you get for a month — then go back and read all the appreciation you have received
- find a place to escape reality (sometimes)
- learn to do one thing at a time
- get back up when life throws you
- the mark of a moderate person is freedom from her own ideas
- sit on your heels with knees and feet together for ten minutes after a meal to aid digestion
- use mudras (hand postures) in combination with breathing exercises, visualization, and affirmation to attain inner peace and quiet
- keep asking questions and seeking the answers
- do instead of try; persistence is the hallmark of belief

- meditate at the same time in the same place every day, if possible
- remind yourself that there is really no place you have to go and nothing you have to get that can't wait another moment
- skip infomercials, yesterday's news, horoscopes
- allow music to transport you
- trust the knowledge to be there when you need it
- allow yourself to be aware of what is before you
- help someone practice an instrument
- don't blame yourself for your child's failures
- request a special dream
- be a nonconformist
- read Gurmukh's *The Eight Human Talents*
- look for volunteer opportunities that will also help you achieve other life goals
- trust your wits
- make donations

- how much of your hard-earned money gets thrown away on the temporary pleasure of stuff?
- give a business suit to a homeless person who is looking for a job
- read *Good Night, Moon* to a child
- accept your physical limitations
- attend a benefit for a worthy cause
- make a good impression on yourself
- replace old and harmful habits of thought by new constructive ones
- wash someone's car windows — on the inside
- make full use of what happens to you
- spend more time in nature
- surprise a new neighbor with one of your favorite homemade dishes
- read "hints & tips" books
- do the Bow Pose to keep your spine supple, tone your abdomen, and decrease laziness

- sit outside at dusk and watch it get dark
- appreciate the cinema
- let yoga provide answers
- unclutter
- give a teenager a Do Not Disturb sign for his or her room
- investigate your distractions
- be the designated listener
- study tai chi with a qualified teacher
- be careful in all you think and do
- try to have a carefully arranged mind
- one smile can begin a friendship
- be the artist, the writer, the creator of your future
- let your child jump on his or her bed
- put a jacket over someone sleeping in the car
- spot for someone at the gym
- see how rich you are inside
- speak the right words

- take the long view
- try to refrain from drinking during a meal
- go to a beautiful place to sit still and read
- consciously elevate your intentions
- let go of old habits by replacing them with new ones
- realizations come naturally through the process of surrendering
- clear space, literally and figuratively, so there is room for more delight in your life
- take one more step when you don't think you can
- give a tool kit to a couple just starting out
- be honest with each other
- give the gift of a laundry service to new parents
- if you sell anything, offer a money-back refund
- it's never too late to show that you appreciate someone
- treat your hands to a simple acupressure massage
- bear everything to realize everything
- clean your shoe bottoms before going inside

instant karma

- delight in paradox and irony
- contemplate your life
- be able to fill leisure intelligently
- govern the inside, not the outside
- buy a gift that will keep you giggling
- love what you do
- get a paint-by-number kit for an elderly person
- buy paintings by local artists
- find less toxic ways to handle insect infestations
- appreciate new forms of music
- have a Buddha statue across from and facing the door, the position of power and honor
- eat more meatless meals
- be multitalented
- tell someone how you feel and listen to their suggestions, then calmly decide what to do
- see someone through the good, the bad, and the ugly
- do what you mean

- pause sixty seconds before answering a question
- visit someone who would love to see you
- look for the light at the end of the tunnel
- know what to do in emergencies
- breathe in and out three times
  and watch time slow down
- open the windows as you drive and experience
  the tapestry of smells
- listen to your silent voice
- practice yoga right after your shower
- bring a brown-bag lunch on your next flight
- identify the colors that make you happy — wear them
  and decorate with them
- dress sufficiently to cover your body
  and keep out the cold
- try not to eat large meals late at night
- talk with a lonely child
- treat yourself kindly

- quiet your mind by dabbing several drops of lavender oil on a handkerchief and placing it on your pillow
- meet your friends after work
- take an active, positive role in healing your own mind, body, and spirit
- be swift to hear, slow to speak
- celebrate Sweetest Day in October
- take a sacred journey or pilgrimage on foot
- make a survival kit for someone who is sick: favorite magazines, books, *TV Guide,* soup, juices, and a handmade "feel better" card
- call your best friend
- host a meal for others
- give the gift of time and energy
- it's not just what you say — it's how, when, and why you say it
- be your own disciplinarian
- appreciate nonverbal communication

- by letting go, it all gets done
- what matters most is what the mind takes in, feeds on, and puts back out into the world
- allow your heart to remain as open as it feels when you give
- sit and listen quietly to all the sounds of your house that you are not usually aware of
- engage in the basic breathing technique of *pranayama,* which brings oxygen deep into cells and pulls out toxins
- think before you speak
- work toward guaranteed medical care
- giggle with children
- donate an old car to charity
- limit the amount of bingeable food in the house
- carry home your groceries
- imagine yourself behaving and looking and standing as a confident person

- remember that beauty is relative
- you are perfect: your mistakes are lessons; your disappointments are tests
- pull out some old favorite games — Monopoly, Clue, Parcheesi — to play with Mom and Dad
- dispose of auto fluids safely when doing car maintenance
- imagine what your life would be like without your bad habit
- do the thing you like doing most and do it often
- eliminate unnecessary commitments
- make every effort to reconcile and resolve all conflicts, however small
- keep in step
- keep an anti-monster flashlight available for a child
- each moment of nonwanting is a moment of freedom
- every thought, every action, every feeling you have affects your future karma for better or worse

- speak a kind word to some person
- have a firm handshake
- know when to get in the game and when to stay on the sidelines
- do not lie to anyone at all
- let the Buddha speak through you with healing words of acceptance, love, and compassion
- take the family berry picking
- seek out friends or professional help when you feel unable to cope
- take a stress-reduction class
- feel free to question and investigate
- keep your eye on the donut, not on the hole
- keep the kids' toys to a minimum
- say "please"
- focus all your attention on a single person for a whole day
- help outlaw hunting for recreation

- always act as if others were watching
- always know what you are eating and what is eating you
- get involved at your child's school
- listen to inspirational tapes while commuting
- send congratulatory notes
- when washing dishes, be fully aware of each dish, the water, the movement of your hands
- understand what Memorial Day is honoring
- teach intelligent decision making
- cultivate the habit of success
- emulate masters of old, following and respecting their excellent examples
- speak kindly to strangers
- practice *ujjayi*, or drawing breath, to aid in recalling and working with your dreams
- create bedtime stories in which your child is the hero or heroine in an adventure
- the path is reward enough

 439 instant karma

- possess only what is necessary
- look at situations with a balanced point of view
- dance a waltz
- gracefully accept feeling bad, knowing that negative feelings will pass
- cooperate
- three-part breathing is breathing all air out, then filling the belly, rib cage, and collarbone area before breathing out again
- think only and entirely of what you are doing at the moment and you will be free
- be conscious of how you live your life
- keep the small stuff small
- seek out the good in people
- convince a billionaire to become a philanthropist
- excuse blunders
- help women by getting involved with shelters, domestic violence prevention, or victim hotlines

- center and collect yourself each time you speak
- take a soul-cleansing walk in the rain
- cultivate wholesome mental states prior to sleep
- Pain is inevitable but suffering is optional
  (Hermann Witte)
- give people adoring looks
- say prayers for healing and longevity
- read with your dictionary close at hand
- watch out for traffic, hold hands, and stick together
- *you already have everything you need*
- do not kill or cause others to kill
- keep the dharma foremost in mind
- attitude is key to coping with problems
- practice breathing between phone calls
- relinquish the habit of having to be in charge
  or the habit of giving in
- have a "no bed-making" day each week
- add introspection to breath awareness

- do what you really want to do
- become more conscious of what you say and how you say it
- go for a walk to clear your mind and step away from the responsibilities of home, work, and/or school
- conserve your energy
- sing along with anything cheerful, even in the grocery store or at a restaurant
- buy a handbag on eBay rather than pay full price for one in a store
- instead of exchanging family gifts, provide Christmas for a needy family
- the mind should be filled with dharma talk: righteous talk, talk that uplifts, talk that helps, talk that soothes
- have rules for children that are fair and consistent
- karma yoga is the yoga of right and selfless action
- take it as a given that others will do things differently and react differently to the same situation

- remind yourself to work at letting go of ego-clinging, selfishness, possessiveness, aggression, resentment, confusion
- try to share in pilgrimages, prayers, and meditations at the holy places of different faiths
- learn to be free, willing to take reasonable risks, open to others and new ideas
- give a kid a magazine subscription
- tip the strolling troubadours
- you can make the place you are now your paradise
- between errands, spend private time in the car reading
- reduce your vices and increase your virtues
- learn the art of being silly
- donate books to a psychiatric ward
- volunteer for overnight duty at a shelter
- believe in others' potential and help them realize it
- act like a tourist
- learning is the way to change your life

- be happy with what you have while working for what you want
- use Julie Morgenstern's SPACE organizing method: Sort, Purge, Assign a home, Containerize, Equalize
- help a child learn about and understand history
- when you feel unsure of your direction, do an "I am" affirmation mantra/meditation
- strive most to understand what you fear most
- don't miss a thing!
- create a more self-sufficient lifestyle
- buy your child a present on Mother's Day in return for him making you a mother
- let go of fixed plans and concepts
- place a phone call to a friend you have not heard from in a while
- hold hands in the movies
- stop one heart from breaking
- be ready when someone throws you a curve

- honor your innate dignity
- support minority businesses
- be humble and polite
- jump off the bandwagon
- improve your attitude toward one person or situation in your life
- stop your mate in the middle of shaving to give a surprise shaving-cream kiss
- help maintain school playground equipment
- take responsibility for what you do
- when friends offer to help, let them
- love your age
- when you breathe out, know you are breathing out; when you breathe in, know you are breathing in
- give your seat to an elderly person
- take a flashlight wherever you go
- remember the pleasure of working
- aim to do everything smoothly and gracefully

- understand that lessons are life's way of making you change
- rest in the present
- why rush through some moments to get to other "better" ones?
- change from a self-centered to a spirit-centered way of being
- sit on the floor and play with your children
- pursue happiness in every corner of your life
- ask your child if he or she would like to learn something
- ignore the faults of others
- shed ambition
- paint recipe cards with watercolors as gifts for friends
- look for what you need in places where it can be found
- slip a love note into the book your mate is reading
- volunteer at a hospice
- start an herb garden

- be a bookworm
- adapt monastic practices of contentment
- take kids to hands-on museums
- seek harmony
- receive inspiration by studying writings that describe the path to liberation
- discourage gambling
- get a child a journal to record his or her thoughts
- make valentine pillows for everyone you love
- take the time to point someone in the right direction when they are lost
- lower your cholesterol
- celebrate gray hairs
- encourage privacy for children
- use red in rooms with lots of activity or to promote passion
- praise your teammates
- awaken to a favorite aroma

- load up a college kid with prepaid phone cards
- take artistic license
- have the patience to unknot chains and shoelaces
- save before you spend
- have nothing and live in freedom
- clean up your own mess
- be aware of the ways your attitudes affect your physical state
- travel lightly to maintain your vitality
- show respect for others' opinions
- answer a letter promptly
- the path is the goal
- contribute in some way to the larger community
- truth cannot be found through debate or disputation
- read books about how things work
- make a list when you have a lot to do
- bend like tropical palms
- develop some business sense

- practice *tonglen*, sending and taking, breathing in the suffering of the world and breathing out peace and happiness
- practice means being in the present on purpose
- scribble down your thoughts as you have them
- honey can boost your power and endurance
- give a gardener a kneeler stool or pad
- get involved in gardening, crossword puzzles, and other naturally grounding activities
- shop in downtown areas rather than in malls
- dive in without paying attention to resistance
- define what is important and ignore what is not
- improve the environment through cleanups, advocacy, and education
- seek elegance rather than luxury
- do no harm to others and you will find happiness
- hold someone as you fall asleep
- see your body not as yourself but as your vehicle

- slip a quarter in every jukebox you pass
- donate blood
- plant a tree
- express yourself completely, then keep quiet
- find better ways to cope
- go to events at your local bookstores and library — author talks, storytelling, reading clubs
- reuse an old bridesmaid dress
- leave a legacy of good feelings
- the more things you plan to do, the more energy you'll have
- improve your inner beauty
- put all the happiness you can into each moment
- teach manners in grade school
- talk heart-to-heart with someone who needs it
- experiment with consciously choosing to miss a meal
- offer a genuine hello and a smile to people you meet
- be completely present

- around other people, don't think about yourself
- when you go with pain, the pain passes quickly
- succeed in not raising your voice during a fight
- do not live in a hurry
- your words should carry conviction
- actively choose to be positive
- put on the soundtrack of a favorite Broadway show and sing in the shower
- walk to boost your spirits
- discipline is not deprivation — it is self-care
- if you find yourself losing interest, refocus
- try acupuncture for something that ails you
- pray for a sick child
- shield your sleep from worry by scheduling "worry time" well before bedtime
- block out the unnecessary
- find creative expression
- don't make people wait for you

- buy from farm stands
- travel
- ask questions that let the other person know you were listening closely
- live intensely
- never be discouraged
- make a phone call to tell someone the good thoughts you've had about her
- make your boss look good
- provoke change, but don't try to force it
- articulate your most fundamental beliefs
- clip out articles for your sweetie to read
- wear your hair to suit yourself
- become an opportunist
- cultivate inner and external freedom
- practice unconditional love
- give a great dictionary, thesaurus, almanac, and atlas to a kid going to college

- plan your purchases
- infuse your life with new perspectives on prosperity
- don't say, "I told you so"
- create your own recipes
- take the time to know someone's heart and show them yours
- quiet your mind through silent prayer
- don't put other people down
- savor an achievement
- take a deep breath and imagine that you are pulling your energy back into your body; you will immediately feel more grounded, centered, powerful
- strive for progress, not perfection
- help your child get organized, especially with school stuff
- be the first one to act loving or reach out
- smile even when you have reason to complain
- put a candy under someone's pillow

 instant karma

- walk/exercise/move
- boycott poor workmanship and poor work ethic
- turn on a passenger's favorite radio station
- love, even when hate is all around you
- be someone's pillow
- meditate in a place of natural beauty if possible
- love learning
- be the first to make up after a disagreement
- the pleasure is always in the process
- keep your favorite subject favorite by not talking about it
- learn the difference between needs and wants
- enjoy a walker's perception
- give a new driver a gift certificate to the local gas station
- constantly strive to improve your education
- take a one-on-one class in the Alexander Technique
- eat fish twice per week

- surprise kids with an ice cream stop
- spend as long as necessary listening to someone talk about what's troubling them
- explore yourself and the world with consciousness and compassion
- on a rainy evening, write long letters or e-mails to old friends
- let your regrets gather dust
- be with people you like and who make you happy
- love a thing for its own sake
- acknowledge even small improvements
- put a space heater in the garage for Dad
- spruce up a local park
- while listening, don't fidget
- knowledge of your own mortality is the greatest gift God could ever give you
- Revere the healing power of nature (Hippocrates)
- give your best to every activity

- use curiosity as the best cure for disappointments
- allow sound into your home — wind chimes, water, birds, etc.
- check e-mail at set times rather than letting each new message interrupt you
- bury the hatchet with an old friend
- try not to add anything unnecessary or extraneous to your life
- ride your bicycle to the local farm store
- jot down any compliments you get and read them when you're feeling down
- distract someone who is getting an immunization
- preserve vegetation for wild animals' food
- it's never too late
- the only real control you have is choice of your own thoughts, your own words, and your own actions
- put a small bunch of flowers in a glass and place them by a child's bed

- try new ingredients and cooking styles
- practice the Seven-Point Posture (sensing the legs, arms, back, eyes, jaw, tongue, head in a sitting position) to gain a calm, clear state of mind
- end each day with a hug
- think big thoughts
- stop trying to impress other people
- hang laundry to dry on a wash line to conserve energy
- live off the food you already have in your pantry
- shop with a list
- schedule morning workouts
- prepare a wonderful dinner for Mom
- just do what must be done
- shovel the snow from the driveway and then build a snowman
- buy recycled paper; reuse paper that is printed only on one side
- open up, dive in, be free

- renew your faith by reading inspirational literature
- work with neighbors on a common problem
- visit a warm climate to help wintertime blues
- make meals your family loves
- the people you associate with influence the direction of your life
- stretch beyond what is comfortable
- make a wish for the day each morning
- send an anniversary telegram
- when you see someone possessed of beauty, wealth, or happiness, rejoice for them
- want what you have
- see the forest and the trees
- walk in something soft with bare feet
- Zen is concerned only with direct experience, either of the intuition or on the physical plane
- provide a good home library for your children
- trust that you will be taken care of

- if you have flashes of brilliance when you are showering, walking, driving, take the time to write them down
- let go of a self-limiting belief
- flex your risk muscle
- know that all news is biased
- participate in a Race for the Cure for breast cancer
- attempt to create a state in which you are always present
- keep technology in its place
- sponsor a kids' sports team
- the way out of a trap is to study the trap itself: learn how it is built, take it apart piece by piece
- take photos, tuck away keepsakes
- meditate on the cycle of the sun as a visual metaphor for the human life span
- when your back is up against the wall, lean on it and relax

- Make the most of yourself, for that is all there is to you (Ralph Waldo Emerson)
- lie in a hammock and look at the treetops
- take time to develop shared goals with your mate
- become a Lamaze coach for a single mom
- Your visions will become clear only when you can look into your own heart. Who looks outside, dreams; who looks inside, awakes. (Carl Jung)
- be unprejudiced
- a smile will help you start being a part-time Buddha right now
- cultivate ambidexterity
- play jazz or classical music during brainstorming and breaks
- act courteously
- buy less
- looking for lasting happiness outside yourself is like expecting to get in shape by watching others exercise

- meet your needs, skip desires
- speak positively and your thoughts will follow suit
- learn yogic breathing and do it daily
- look for a gradual and continual change in yourself
- step aside when others are quarreling
- stare out the window daydreaming
- feed a stranger's expired parking meter
- watch the wind
- look beyond the wisdom accepted as reality and begin to understand the Truth
- keep your bedroom slightly cool to help you sleep better
- practice relaxation after hours of hard work
- make sure you are compensated fairly for your work
- have faith in the way things are
- in Pilates, do each move with control and follow through with precision
- let go of unrealistic fears

461 instant karma

- if you refuse to accept anything but the best out of life, you very often get it
- exercise with a friend
- take a nap every Sunday
- appreciate those moments that go beyond words
- defend others if their rights are being violated
- if something new is available to you, try it instead of saying "I won't" or "I can't"
- when your energy is flagging, lie on your back and put your feet up on a chair, legs bent at a right angle
- read the Great Books
- do one-legged forward bends to tone the abdomen, liver, spleen, and kidneys
- give someone a yo-yo
- wait and trust and you will be shown the solution
- practice where you are
- the meaning of your life is not found in a few great deeds but in thousands of little ones

- admire yourself
- Take time for all things (Ben Franklin)
- don't spend your life looking forward to being somewhere else
- balance the forces of yin and yang
- savor good moments
- don't skip breakfast
- dangle your feet in a fountain
- liberate yourself from the indulgent, material world
- talk back to self-doubt
- help a student buy a ticket home for the holidays
- find one place outside where you feel you can be by yourself and reflect on life
- focus on the enjoyment of a game, not winning
- champion local industries
- realize that the journey to the center takes place within your own mind
- give love

- cleanse through a meager diet, silence, and journal writing
- pick a personal sanctuary in your home
- leave everything a little better than you found it
- look at all the good in the world and try to give some of it back
- find meaning in random ideas
- bake a surprise chocolate cake for the kids
- let change feel good
- inside each of us is a core of essential goodness and purity
- think in terms of gray rather than black and white
- allow yourself to feel rich without money
- meditation is the balance of awareness, concentration, and energy
- spend no time assigning blame, no energy in accusation
- end the day with chamomile tea

instant karma 464

- have a home that your children's friends love to visit
- take delight in the richness of language
- dig deeper
- pick out a card and send it to someone who would never expect it
- do neurobics (brain exercises)
- when you change yourself, you often find that the change you desired in others happens as well
- be the salt of the earth
- figure out what your pain is trying to tell you
- buy a cool walking stick for someone who needs it
- teach your kids from an early age to enjoy quiet time
- do something fun every single day
- do your own thing
- consider a different point of view
- the way of Zen is to clean as you go
- stand up for yourself and your beliefs
- tell your best joke

- stop thinking and end your problems
- get college credit for your life experience
- notice what's happening in your head before your thoughts have a chance to build momentum
- let a child grow carnivorous plants to learn some basic botany
- decide, then persevere
- keep learning new skills, try new hobbies
- do less acquiring and pay more attention to what you already have
- be so busy you don't have time to search for happiness
- have work to do and be content with the work
- assist in the birth of a baby
- leave store coupons near the coupon items on supermarket shelves
- get involved with people outside your usual circle of friends
- tell your children about yourself

- memorize Buddhism's Five Remembrances: there is no way to escape growing old, having ill health, death, being separated from all that is, and the consequences of your actions
- cultivate an attitude of nonchalance to extremes
- do one new thing each week
- examine your conscience
- learn to see through your opinions and perceive things as they actually are
- during your travels, carry your sense of "place" within yourself
- make your own holiday cards
- know when to keep silent; know when to speak up
- feel at home wherever you are
- throw a welcome party
- ask with absolute sincerity and the way opens
- invest free time in your partner, children, friends
- consume more antioxidants

467 instant karma

- be soft when your impulse is to be hard, generous when your impulse is to be withholding, open when your impulse is to shut down emotionally
- take off the blinders
- do yoga twists to realign your spine
- counting steps in Zen walking turns off the stream of distracting thoughts
- sit in a rocker, listening to the silence and reflecting
- whenever you purchase something new, give something away
- clean up your own room
- golf with your dad
- make a list of the ten most beautiful things you have ever experienced in any way
- use an answering machine more often
- drive a friend to her doctor appointments
- take one step forward and no steps back
- be understanding

- don't take life that seriously — it is here to be enjoyed
- enjoy fall yard work
- make sure you get at least one hug a day
- make peace with yourself once and for all
- forget what others think of you
- bear unhappiness with courage
- take a course at a botanical garden
- when someone hurts you and you don't react,
  you are beginning to show wisdom and intelligence
- let people pull in front of you in a traffic jam
- barter for picking privileges in a neighbor's
  organic garden
- hold on to good; avoid every kind of evil
- cultivate a diverse group of friends
- get up with the sunrise each morning
- do something unusual on your lunch hour
- mental calmness is a very important factor for
  good health

- tell the truth and accept the consequences
- you can recover yourself completely after three breaths
- remember that the clock is a human invention
- dare to live the life you have dreamed for yourself
- agree with criticism directed toward you and see how this can defuse the situation
- stop a compulsion
- allow children to take risks and get dirty
- mouth "I love you" across a room
- plunge into new things: it's the only way to grow and change
- listen to the sounds and voices of the world
- adopt an abandoned kitten
- go to your high school reunion and have fun
- read all the books you never made time for before
- listen to customers
- spend a Saturday morning with the kids, watching cartoons, relaxing in pajamas with a bowl of cereal

- smile at law enforcement officers
- of two evils, choose neither
- seek out quiet places: a garden, a reading room in a library, a corner nook in a café, a botanical garden, a chapel, a rotunda at a museum, a terrace, a hammock
- lower your family's energy consumption
- inhale negative karma, difficulties, conflicting emotions; exhale it as happiness and joy
- have fun with friends or family at least once a week
- consider never weighing yourself; see how clothes fit and how you feel as a more reliable indicator
- have a well-wishing attitude
- seek and ye shall find
- put trouble into a boat of leaves and sail it out to sea
- realize the difference between the annoying and the tragic
- practice hugging meditation, breathing in and out three times

 instant karma

- whenever possible, avoid eating in a hurry
- ask thoughtful questions
- jog with a friend
- live each daylight hour with depth, concentration, and focus
- learn to do some maintenance and service for your car
- choose one fun thing to look forward to each day
- be an advocate of home cooking
- shift your focus from what isn't working to what is
- delight in the experience of waking up
- listen to your inner hum
- gaze at a candle flame from about two feet away as a meditation technique
- prevent your children from becoming self-centered
- instead of hanging up on a telemarketer, just say, "I am not interested, but thank you for calling"
- decide you want a happy ending and try to make your dream a reality

- give the baby-sitter a checklist and phone numbers
- drink water while you exercise
- appreciate the effort of all hands, both seen and unseen, who labored to put food on the table
- close your eyes and visualize the Oneness of It All
- call your parents on your birthday to thank them for giving you the gift of life
- balanced foods have equal yin and yang: local vegetables, beans, seeds, nuts, fish, and many whole grains
- try to bring microscopic clarity of attention to all your interactions
- place a thin pillow at the small of your back to encourage sitting up straight
- notice the constancy of inner devotion
- avoid changing your sleeping hours dramatically from one day to the next — the body likes routines
- help preserve old buildings

- choose a mantra like *om*
- marvel at how the body works
- hang inspiring art on the walls
- great good is often born of one small act of kindness
- feel the presence of the divine within you
- endure all hardships equally, be patient and strong, and never give in to anger
- when the going gets tough — laugh
- write the words *What Am I Doing?* on a piece of paper and hang it where you will see it often
- sacred words of any language can be used in mantra practice
- mend your mood without food
- take one day each month to visit local art galleries
- imagine yourself as a pitcher pouring out your love to all around you, but remember that you too sometimes need an emotional refill
- eat some fruit every day

- give nearby campers your extra firewood
- practice the Triangle, or Happy Pose, to fill your body with joy and radiate it from within you
- choose warming and stimulating yang foods in fall and winter
- the foods that are healthiest for the human body are also the healthiest for our environment and create the least suffering for other creatures
- subdue your mind
- have a selective library
- organize a neighborhood yard sale
- think of things you can do to balance your work, leisure, and family life
- when you exercise, your reward is more energy and greater strength
- if you want to be quiet and strong, work to improve your faith
- bring morning coffee and juice to guests

 475 Instant karma

- be generous with your lighting; light is happiness
- cultivate a beautiful state of mind
- If you want to be happy, be (Henry David Thoreau)
- make every move count; pick your target and hit it
- there is no destiny or fate — keep the future as free and open as possible
- live by Buddhism's precept of Right Thought and refuse to assume anything about anyone
- use your power and authority gently
- pet a pet
- put difficulty in perspective and ask what choices you have
- feel supremely happy
- give all-over kisses that say, "I could eat you up!"
- keep up with the light housekeeping
- relay an overheard compliment; forget an overheard criticism
- avoid unnecessary tinkering, especially with computers

- consider each word carefully before you say anything so that your speech is "right" in both form and content
- nurture your mind with great thoughts
- nothing happens before its designated time
- search for the middle ground in all things
- dress up to stay at home
- do something to improve your health each day
- clean out your hard drive seasonally
- hold the elevator doors for others
- give a child a real-life adventure
- do not praise yourself
- if you encounter a person of rare intellect, ask him or her what books he or she reads
- if you want to go far each year, you have to make sure that you do something significant each day
- do the Taoist circle walk (*ba gua*) to increase longevity
- look at people when they speak to you
- ignore the silver lining; use the cloud

- a true practitioner of dharma should be like a bee that is never attracted to just one flower but flies from one to another
- concentrate on your exhalation; make it as long and smooth as possible
- To affect the quality of the day, that is the highest of arts (Henry David Thoreau)
- pick up plastic that might choke fish or birds
- appreciate when babies don't cry
- do not think the knowledge you possess is changeless, absolute truth
- tuck the kids in
- choose cooling yin foods in spring and summer
- fill your house with the welcoming smells of nourishing food
- exhibit self-reliance
- be willing to try a new yoga pose, however difficult it seems

- continually analyze and observe yourself
- understand the futility of seeking fulfillment in things that by their nature do not last
- take a specified amount of time each day for meditation, prayer, journal writing, or inspirational reading
- pick up pearls of wisdom from unlikely sources
- go for a walk with the kids or a stroll with the pup
- pretend you are a butterfly floating on the breeze
- each of us is endowed with Buddhism's Five Great Blessings: happiness, health, virtue, peace, and longevity
- there is nothing gained from letting yourself become adversarial with your loved ones
- if you believe a lucky ritual will help, it probably will
- set deadlines
- live and act from the understanding that all things change

- tell people today how much you love them
- expand the neglected sides of your personality
- fill up your inner holes with something spiritual
- always look at what you have left
- watch your actions; they become habits
- read materials that will help you stay on your chosen path
- protect yourself by remaining tranquil
- never cheat
- help someone solve a riddle
- make sure your lifestyle is consistent with what you say
- when you read your mail, act on it immediately
- make sure you have a will naming a guardian and executor
- weigh the consequences of production, usage, and disposal when choosing goods
- show up to work early
- look after a sibling

- use plants as air purifiers: areca palm, lady palm, Boston fern, English ivy, and the rubber plant
- learn to like yourself better
- give thanks for your friends
- make happy memories for someone else
- assist a struggling bag carrier
- care
- tell people not to give you a gift but rather treat themselves (to a concert, bubble bath, etc.)
- have a repentant tongue — most bad karma is created by speech
- show up on time
- accept not being able to win the approval of everyone you meet
- make sure a baby has books everywhere, even for the bathtub
- The only lasting beauty is the beauty of the heart (Rumi)

- ask family members, sincerely, for their advice
- understand advertising for what it is
- one day per month, have the family do kind and special things for one family member
- seriously consider getting up an hour earlier, to claim time totally for yourself
- use healthy cookbooks
- respect what your body naturally craves with the assumption that it knows what it needs best
- before you go to bed, start a list of things you have been putting off
- do things that bring out your best, most magic self
- if you are going into a situation you feel anxious, tense, or afraid about, tell yourself that you are perfect just as you are
- pass up the next chance to criticize
- receive life's gifts
- put up with fools

- wake your child up with a kiss
- stop to look at even the most mundane objects, which are also things of wonder
- allow yourself a Zen moment
- take time to reflect, to sit by a warm fire, to watch a quiet snowfall with loved ones
- learn from anti-role models
- meditate on a length of prayer beads
- in laboring for others, do it with the same zeal as if it were for yourself
- make a birthday list to help gift-givers
- whistle
- seek to understand before being understood
- identify five comfort foods and make sure you have them available
- refrain from using your horn when driving
- see good conditions as a gift and a blessing, rather than taking them for granted

- Whatever satisfies the soul is truth (Walt Whitman)
- catch more flies with honey than with vinegar
- do muscle relaxation exercises to control stress
- donate 5 percent of your time or income to help the less fortunate
- Remember that it is better not to speak of things you do not understand (*Tao Te Ching*)
- speak up at meetings
- pay off credit cards each month
- rejoice in life, find the world beautiful and delightful to live in
- choose your helpers wisely
- give simple gifts
- attempt to understand our present age and the historical forces shaping it
- take the opportunity to do small things well
- be selective
- act as your inner jester

instant karma 484

- mow the lawn for your father
- offer kids a bag of magic tricks to play with
- try these healthy snacks: raw vegetables, dried fruit, rice cakes
- head a charitable organization
- offer to pay for parking and tolls when you ride in someone else's car
- stamp out bigotry
- thank a friend who believes in you
- pledge a significant contribution to your local National Public Radio station
- leave a great magazine in the doctor or dentist's waiting room
- be ready for an epiphany
- help create alternatives for landfills
- try not to let things bother you
- love the journey, not the destination
- work with good tools

- do an apprenticeship
- pay employees well
- transcend predicaments with laughter
- be audaciously present
- the gentle chanting of *ah* is a smooth, openhearted meditation
- start your day with an invigorating practice of Sun Salutation
- overtip breakfast waitresses
- how you speak to yourself can have a powerful effect on what happens in your life
- have a humble abode
- in family life, be completely present
- stay in contact with family and friends
- let children see you and your partner kiss each other
- let the past stay there
- lift people up
- experience the ease of relatively unencumbered living

- Buddhism's *metta* prayer: May all beings be happy, content, and fulfilled. May all beings be healed and whole. May all have whatever they need. May all beings be protected from harm and freed from fear. May all enjoy inner peace and ease. May all be awakened, liberated, and free. May there be peace in this world and universe.
- motive is more important than technique
- avoid arrogance
- have a love affair with life
- develop a multicultural perspective
- learn to be genuine in every moment of your life
- shop for shut-ins
- support your family; stand together
- let your spiritual side guide your material side, not the other way around
- brighten up even the tiniest corners of your world
- take a therapeutic stroll on a beach

instant karma

- make sure there is a warm throw rug for cold feet
- set mini-goals and work on them every day
- paint bathrooms in earth tones
  (yellow, tan, orange, brown)
- everything you need to break unhealthy cycles
  of behavior is within you
- pay off your student loans
- find a way to get involved in politics and government
- perform an old American wedding custom, the
  shivaree (a mock serenade with pots, pans, and
  cowbells) outside the newlyweds' window
- love yourself for who you are
- don't give others what they don't want
- preserve antique or old childhood books
- be grateful for your memories and reflect on how time
  has been good to you
- drop altogether the idea of security and see the irony
  of your attempts to secure yourself

- plan a visit "back home"
- try brain expansion work, where you balance the use of both sides of your brain
- persevere through the innumerable ups and downs of the path
- live as though you have nothing to lose
- give honest and sincere appreciation
- allow more light to flow through you
- study hard, think quietly, talk gently, act frankly
- do things that give you energy
- conserve water voluntarily
- be willing to experience discomfort in the pursuit of a dream
- get rid of things that distract your attention
- put the energy of anger into cleaning a room, washing the dishes, straightening a closet
- get someone a briefcase for starting a new job
- take risks with people

- free your weekends for your family if you are busy with work the rest of the week
- keep public places clean
- when circumstances cannot be changed, change yourself
- be a nice person
- notice a harsh thought and count to ten before reacting or responding
- watch the moon rise
- voraciously transform all of life, family, job, good and bad, everything, into dharma
- hire a former welfare recipient
- make exercise nonnegotiable
- come prepared to work hard each day
- be grateful for all you have, even if it's not enough
- learn the value of fantasy
- imagine your anger is leaving your body and melting away into the ground or water

instant karma 490

- read a book, feeling the words were written just for you
- get in touch with your body by using the Feldenkrais method
- keep visualization positive and realistic and multisensory
- live for something bigger than you
- share with others how important they are to you
- never compromise your dreams
- phone if you can't make a personal appearance on a birthday
- love is an unselfish attitude, not an attachment
- accompany an ethnic meal with appropriate ethnic music
- you only need what will make your life better and happier, not what will weigh it down
- be early to appointments
- when another person makes you suffer, it is because he suffers deeply within himself

 instant karma

- learn how to stop talking when there is nothing more to say
- plan moonlit walks with someone
- refrain from defending your reputation or intentions
- walk a country mile on a summer day
- live consciously, not on automatic pilot
- practice *dana* (giving), to become happier, freer, more content
- be alone without feeling lonely
- if you commute, look into car sharing
- accept the other person's point of view and value that he or she has communicated it to you
- purposefully stop all the doing in your life
- practice *bodhicitta:* think of others as being more important than you are
- realize that what you're looking for is already here
- be your child's greatest advocate
- concentrate on every single thing you do

- clean the tub or shower drain for others
- treat yourself to a massage
- letting go a little improves life; letting go a lot brings happiness and joy
- do something that requires much gathering of courage
- sniff a hankie dipped in essential oils to stave off four o'clock blood-sugar-drop cravings
- learn to be independent and not make others dependent on you
- empower yourself without overpowering others
- be completely alert: never neglectful, never indulgent
- write positive inspirational thoughts in a quote book
- contribute a percentage of your income to charity
- applaud any improvement in willpower
- leave a quarter or two near the jukebox for someone
- try to achieve a yin/yang, light/dark balance in your garden
- spend one day a month in solitude

- resist the temptation to give up when your hoped-for
  goal doesn't materialize quickly
- most of the time, you are probably more hungry
  for breath than you are for food
- dream as if you'll dream forever; live as if you'll
  die today
- give a sudden hug when passing someone in the house
- whenever objects of attraction or aversion arise,
  meditate on the emptiness of both
- inspire children to live life to the fullest
- visualize your body holding a yoga pose, become one
  with the pose
- bicycle to get supplies and the mail
- try eating fish to improve your concentration
- hold it all in until you've figured out how
  to say something in a useful way
- count your blessings
- prepare a breakfast from another country

- Cultivate peace of mind which does not separate one's self from one's surroundings. When that is done successfully, then everything else follows naturally. (Robert M. Pirsig)
- take a deep breath and move on
- send a "Thinking of You" card to someone who really needs it
- find something to smile about every day
- practice zazen by counting your breath, one for each inhale and exhale, up to ten, then back to one
- treasure your mind, cherish your reason, hold to your purpose
- do deep relaxation with your head and shoulders on a pillow to open your chest — and a blanket over you for warmth
- Never doubt that a small group of thoughtful, committed citizens can change the world. Indeed, it is the only thing that ever has. (Margaret Mead)

- resolve not to minimize someone else's problems
- vote in the primary
- dwell among the beauties and mysteries of the earth
- have the good sense to stop when tired
- do something that gives you a glow
- fix a snack to share
- make fresh juice
- practice Child's Pose to stimulate respiration
  by compressing your diaphragm
- sleep with the window open to add luster to
  your complexion
- let your body feel completely at ease and natural
  every moment
- guard your private time as your most treasured asset
- learn some form of shorthand for better note-taking
- deliver acceptance instead of judgment, love instead
  of hate
- take a cooking class with someone you love

- refrain from chronic caretaking
- use pain rather than resist it
- put your partner in the spotlight; be his or her champion
- be willing to learn what you need to know
- be a good parent: show up, listen, try to laugh
- provide a safe hangout for teenagers
- drink a glass of water before every meal
- drive someone to school when it is raining
- prepare children for adulthood
- realize that being who you want to be and doing what you want to do is self-respect
- look before you leap
- help your mate realize his or her dream
- start off the day with warm-from-the-oven pastries
- tell people about suggestions they offered that helped you
- serve your kids breakfast in bed

- clean up the kitchen as soon as you finish eating the meal, while you still have the energy
- seek cleanliness in your body, clarity in your mind, and purity in your soul
- stay curious
- do your shopping in the neighborhood
- accept that pain and disappointment are part of life
- whenever your mind tries to dwell on negative information, take time to silently clear your head
- question your most comfortable assumptions
- whistle when you're feeling down
- simplify household routines
- appreciate a three-year-old's imagination
- dedicate your life to something
- watch the spreading ripples as a coin lands in the center of a pond
- make a "cheer up" basket for a friend
- finish the sentence, "I want to explore . . . "

instant karma 498

- get rid of excuses
- unplug the phone when it is family time
- be a first-rate version of yourself, not a second-rate imitation of someone else
- meet a group of senior citizens for checkers in the park on Sunday afternoon
- tell your family if you feel under mental strain
- what is important is not the quantity of your knowledge, but its quality
- buy a lottery ticket for a loved one
- practice *asanas* (yoga poses) to learn to exercise self-control
- it's not what happens to you that matters most; it's what you do with it
- keep communication open with every member of your family
- use your ability to persist
- be a can-do and a will-try person

- respect every person, no matter how miserable or ridiculous he or she may be
- set aside time for relaxation
- be an example of a person with integrity
- expand your mind and perspective through reading
- be gentle in your criticism and encouraging in your praise
- never underestimate the power of love, the power of forgiveness, the power of a kind word or deed
- the entire art of meditation is knowing how to begin again
- regularly borrow library books
- eat at least half your calories by early afternoon
- avoid contradicting people
- use yellow to stimulate the left side of the brain
- let a kid stay up really late on a special day
- send your parents to the Hawaiian Islands for their fiftieth anniversary

- give evil nothing to oppose and it will disappear by itself
- support telecommuting
- look at the amusing side
- let your eyes be soft and relaxed
- try the Standing Stabilizer for abdominals
- put on boots and tramp through wet fields and woods to remind yourself of all the things that were buried or forgotten in winter
- accept the limitations of being human, but know that your spirit will ultimately transcend those limits
- shop with canvas or net bags
- dress for pleasure
- play
- never give up on what you really want to do
- trust your subconscious to nudge you when you should wake from a nap
- visit an Amish village and appreciate its simple lifestyle

 instant karma

- set things in order
- try balneotherapy (bathing therapy), thalasotherapy (showers and soaking rituals using marine products), full-body wraps, herbal soaks, steam treatments, and dips in mud pits
- savor life's small moments
- take advantage of all the opportunities to keep your mouth shut
- use full-spectrum lightbulbs
- make a "costume" collection for a little girl from old clothes
- for a few moments (or longer!) each day, allow yourself to stop striving and free yourself from worry
- learn to juggle; it develops mind-body coordination
- enjoy the quiet spirit of holiday music
- smile for no reason
- do everything with a mind that lets go
- do standing pelvic tilts to open up the second chakra

- always let conscience be your guide
- take a walk in the woods with a field guide; discover trees, animals, and birds
- be an affable person
- let your words be straight, simple, and said with a smile — you are what you say
- release, give up your individuality, and merge with the Tao
- recognize the good qualities in your children
- keep fire extinguishers handy
- remember that not getting what you want is sometimes a stroke of good luck
- at the end of the day, give a prayer of thanks
- give vegetarianism a try for two solid months
- know your chief asset and cultivate it
- experiment with humor, creativity, and compassion on your job
- give up your certainty that you are right

- take everything out of your closet and start over
- the greatest protection is a loving heart
- save one evening a week for just you and your spouse
- recognize the difference between a bad day and a hopeless life
- relax by closing your eyes and counting backwards slowly from 100
- keep your faith a private matter
- wake up the body with Pilates
- wear warm gloves and socks
- learn things together
- sew up scented shoe pillows for family athletes
- do not keep holding on to anything you have done
- behave in your youth in such a way that you can live your old age in peace
- in autumn, meditate on the bounty of nature's gift
- chaperone a school dance
- live life as an experiment

- take nourishment from the sun
- bake a loaf of bread for someone
- develop your own values and beliefs
- manage gracefully
- be grateful to everyone
- make eye contact with people by focusing on one of their eyes
- resist the urge to criticize yourself and others
- gear your thoughts toward what's right with someone
- true giving means letting go of control
- be direct and clear in your communication
- neither scurry nor haste at an early hour
- make sure you can laugh in almost any situation
- giving a gift of bird feathers offers protection
- trust in your capacity to transform with a changing situation
- fill your garden with a variety of flowers
- drink more water

- wave to planes departing from the airport
- remember where you came from and celebrate your ethnicity
- when someone asks you what you want, tell them
- keep pitchers of water with sliced lemon in the refrigerator
- take a few weeks off from life and just read
- be willing to walk slowly enough for a three-year-old to explore the world
- read the *Tao Te Ching,* which teaches about nature
- tell someone she is beautiful
- eat five fruits and vegetables every day
- end a practice period by saying, "May I be peaceful. May I be happy. May all beings be peaceful. May all beings be happy."
- challenge yourself to higher, more difficult levels
- accept death and go about the business of life with calm

- whatever you have to do, allow a little more time than you think it will take
- appreciate fringe benefits
- create your own merit
- take responsibility for your errors, never placing blame on others
- scrutinize all your thoughts and actions for any trace of nonbeneficial or unwholesome motivation
- try to figure out the meaning of strange words from the context of the sentence
- do no harm
- tackle tough, mind-enriching pursuits
- do leg lifts to strengthen your stomach, which, in turn, supports your lower back
- resist the urge to tell others what they need
- if you are going to laugh about it in ten years, why not laugh now?
- look at the role of food in living a balanced life

- be sustained by inner strength
- when you feel your mind moving too quickly, it is time to back off and regain your bearings
- find beauty in the ordinary and the ordinary in beauty
- break out the satin bedsheets
- pretend that nothing you use can be thrown away — and think up alternative uses for what you formerly called garbage
- expose children to different religions and allow them to choose their path
- be generous, offer compliments, give accurate feedback, listen carefully
- steady your wavering thoughts before you act
- give your mate a book of love poems
- ask, "What is the best that could happen?"
- be open to others' insights and experiences
- a 20-minute meditation can help you see things afresh
- say hello to everyone you meet

- deal with your stress by learning new methods: breathing, getting a change of scene, a hot bath
- count a different blessing every day
- believe in yourself when no one else will
- To look up is joy (Confucius)
- start someone's day off with their favorite breakfast
- in feng shui, burning a yellow candle promotes calm and intelligence
- work to have no hidden jealousies, desires, or angers
- avoid snacks between meals
- don't drink and drive
- try listening to yourself so you can hear how you sound from a different perspective
- periodically do it someone else's way
- know you have the power to achieve what you dream
- don't try to do too much too quickly
- without being perfect, you will do just fine
- make your own declaration of independence

- practice Butterfly Pose to open your hips and the pelvic chakra
- if angry drivers want to pass you in haste, let them; where they're going is not the way
- recall the most thoughtful gesture you received last year and perpetuate the kindness by doing it for someone else
- what is rightly yours will come to you
- appreciate being served by a friendly, helpful person
- remember all the sweet things in your life
- boost energy by climbing stairs
- learn sign language for "I love you"
- for anger, establish a *metta* (loving-kindness) meditation practice
- don't burn bridges
- give a rose plant to someone for Valentine's Day
- clean out your wallet, makeup case, and pocketbook
- be bold in life

- when your acts are motivated by generosity, love, or wisdom, you are creating karmic conditions for abundance and happiness
- establish a network of trustworthy teachers, mentors, or trainers who can help you map out and stick to a path
- make homemade "TV dinners" for the freezer for nights you'll be out
- it is not how you look to the world that matters, but how you act
- work on a parade float
- research the causes and issues important to you
- give your partner a foot rub
- appreciate competence
- simplify your kids' wardrobes
- learn to see all the phenomena in the mind as being perfectly natural and understandable
- designate a day as Giving-Away Day

- work
- let a child bang on pots and pans if they're crabby
- drive an elderly person to a beauty shop appointment
- with mindfulness, you treasure your happiness
  and can make it last longer
- the next time someone at the office or at home
  is looking for help, offer to pitch in
- laugh long and loudly
- do something without being asked
- be part of the solution
- change what is not working
- use a softer tone of voice
- see an outdoor concert
- attain happiness, freedom, and peace of mind
  by giving them to someone else
- donate for the preservation of historic landmarks
- be physically and emotionally available
  for your loved ones

- know when to call a doctor
- take more three-day weekends
- renovate a house yourself
- give thanks before and after meals — or at least pause and be grateful
- give up on logic; listen to that voice inside you
- hang a prism in a baby's room
- let go of your perfectionism
- save money
- campaign for civil rights
- do the Modified Cobra Pose to stretch the lower spine
- read ancient wisdom
- leave a small gift or bouquet on someone's desk at work
- remember that your character matters more than your reputation
- recognize that it is your own ego that causes embarrassment, not a situation

- doubt if you must — but persist
- call people by their preferred names
- imagine a pleasant breeze flowing over you and taking your worries as it drifts away
- accept yourself, warts and all — unconditionally
- avoid smoked meats and fish, sausages, and processed meats
- become a minimalist
- sing in the rain
- react pleasantly
- make an effort to experience the validity of information through insight in your daily life
- leave a full cookie jar for kids
- recycle greeting cards as bookmarks
- grocery shop with a list
- keep a "lighten-up" prop, like funny-nose glasses, to put on when things get tense
- devote yourself to lifelong learning

- do less controlling and pay more attention
  to letting go
- kiss your spouse good night and say "I love you"
- learn your job and find the fun parts
- when everything is clear in your own mind,
  nobody can create obstacles for you
- load the different parts of your life onto
  a balancing scale until you see them balance
- do sand-casting with a youngster
- unpack your resentments and just enjoy yourself
- if you can't control it, let it go
- clear your mind with a mini-meditation
- create your own secret hideaway
- donate to a friend's favorite charity
- visit monkeys at zoos
- frolic
- use chopsticks to avoid eating too quickly or
  putting too much food in your mouth

- make time for the things that are important to you
- take pride in your work
- let the sun shine in
- be concerned more with how you live than with how long
- buy produce without plastic or foam packaging
- bide your time
- believe that perseverance is the essential ingredient for personal achievement
- learn from all, judge no one, be kind to all, and say thank you
- try to work things out on your own
- work for the welfare of others
- make the world your research center
- drop your leftover change into a charity can
- do the Frog Pose, which alternates from a squat to a forward bend, 11 to 26 times
- repay your parents however you can

- light a candle for world peace
- a relationship free of unrealistic grasping is free of disappointment, conflict, and jealousy
- make decisions to benefit more than just yourself
- get ready to go on time so you don't delay others
- prolong the spring of early love
- become mindful of your relationship to food
- be respectful to public employees
- to get the best of an argument, avoid it
- walk a dog for a sick neighbor
- bring home a flower or bouquet for your child
- focus on taking control of the choices you make
- choose yogurt over ice cream
- plan a detoxification treatment at least once a year
- escape the winter blahs
- get a small gift for brand-new neighborhood babies upon their arrival
- carry your own bags

- practice *agape:* overflowing love that seeks nothing in return
- know that things turn out best for the people who make the best of the way things turn out
- replace the smoke alarm batteries regularly
- a gift of a jade dove bestows best wishes for health and longevity
- call to tell your family if you are delayed or your plans change
- wash your hands before you eat
- part of our journey is learning to keep only what was good and nurturing in our upbringing, while forgiving the rest
- inspire each other
- remember the important and forget the unimportant
- give a child a chess set to start them early in lessons of strategy and discipline
- invest your money

- do not try to understand or explain everything
- jot down sentences you like when you read them
- give up your tennis court early to someone who has waited awhile
- make friends with an elderly neighbor
- remember the joy of organizing
- teach kids that living by rules is good for them
- obey traffic lights and laws
- get your kids to do as much as they can, for a sense of accomplishment
- begin anew by throwing away old things
- take a brown-bag lunch to the nearest park bench, zoo, duck pond, or warm library steps
- use thoughts and words of love since everything you think and speak comes back to you
- stop yelling
- keep bathroom decor simple
- be gentle with the earth

519 instant karma

- keep maps in your car
- create an unhurried morning routine
- acknowledge the lessons your soul needs to learn
- fulfill the dreams of a child who isn't yours
- concentrate fully on a food's flavor
- use an ionizer to keep the air filled with negatively charged ions — just as in nature
- a sincere "You're doing a great job" can make someone's day
- turn on a favorite record and dance alone
- remember that no mountain is too big to climb if you do it at your own pace
- make sure your windows are clean to allow fresh *chi* to enter
- volunteer to deliver hot meals to AIDS patients at home
- Learn to be still in the midst of activity and to be vibrantly alive in repose (Mahatma Gandhi)

- put handwritten notes in Christmas cards
- Judge not lest you be judged (Jesus)
- use printed reference books from reliable publishers and authors
- when someone tells you about their goal, point out possibilities, not obstacles
- a good artist lets his intuition lead him wherever it wants
- keep your home repaired and in good order
- give a kid a bulletin board to decorate as she wishes
- live according to your deepest heartfelt values
- your enemies provide you with the opportunity to develop tolerance, patience, and understanding
- let others have their own beliefs
- pay attention to the breath in various parts of the body — diaphragm, nostrils, rib cage, etc.
- remember that your mind is like a garden: it must be tended to prevent overgrowth

- furniture should be placed so you can see people coming or going from a room
- live as you will have wished to have lived when you are dying
- light candles at each meal in winter
- every wakeful step, every mindful act is the path
- wish your enemies well and your heart will lighten
- flatter your mate's mother
- don't expect anything in meditation
- learn a language other than your native one
- know there is a time for all things
- develop a "vision statement" of what you want to be, achieve, or contribute
- send the mayor a note of appreciation
- speak only that which you know yourself, see by yourself, and find by yourself
- learn a new job skill
- join a service club

- stand head to knees (forward bend) to stretch the entire back of your body
- take slower, deeper breaths
- if you draw or write a lot, consider investing in a slanted worktop
- drink good coffee, eat good food
- remember the value of time
- have a friend over for tea and a real talk
- give favorite recipes as a wedding present
- run for the school board
- prepare a home organizer notebook for the benefit of others
- keep telephone calls reasonably brief
- drop a dollar on the street and imagine how lucky the finder will feel
- believe there is joy in getting older
- research your plans thoroughly
- squeeze in friendship moments

 523 instant karma

- be consistent with children
- spend a vacation volunteering at a camp for kids with cancer
- know that your life has purpose and meaning
- let the people in line who look as if they are in a hurry go ahead of you
- ask, "What can I be grateful for right now?"
- make friends with the police
- buy a book for someone who has expressed interest in a new topic
- when you stop at a red light, practice relaxing
- consolidate and compress
- do your part to reduce paperwork
- make your actions count
- turn a source of irritation into an opportunity to be mindful
- when you've done something you're really proud of, give yourself a big hand

- build a fire in the fireplace on a not-fit-for-man-nor-beast winter night
- vary your diet
- allow others to finish speaking before you say anything
- go to the family reunion
- Zen archery is used as a spiritual practice for cultivating inner peace
- give a smile to a stranger
- do everything to bring elegance, order, beauty, and joy into each task you perform
- compliment others on their insights and wisdom
- brush snow off a stranger's car in a parking lot
- what you're looking for is right in front of you
- share a cartoon from *The New Yorker*
- recognize the conditioning of your experiences and work to break out of its limitations
- grow old gracefully
- explode with joy

- one peaceful person can have a profound effect on a household
- send an engagement card to newly affianced friends
- the first step depends on the last and the last step depends on the first
- Buddhism's Right Speech is not indulging in lies, gossip, or other thoughtless talk
- avoid people who try to make you feel guilty
- all that you are is a result of what you have thought
- try new things more often
- watch what you say over the fence
- stick to the budget when planning a party
- play the "I love you more than (fill in the blank)" game
- avoid things that hurt your body
- push yourself beyond your limits, all the time
- abandon all your senses to a field of wildflowers
- know people's nicknames

- learn to stay relaxed and friendly no matter how much stress you feel
- do not respond to those who contradict you
- declare a moratorium on new clothes — try to last a whole season
- follow advice for saving electricity and water
- embrace morality
- animals have karma because they have consciousness and intention, but only humans can mindfully discriminate between wholesome and unwholesome acts
- draw little pictures to amuse others
- keep a dish of candy for coworkers
- use hydrotherapy
- believe that hearts mend
- if you notice that someone else is judging you, don't be quick to agree or internalize the judgment
- eschew workaholism

- put on fresh pajamas each day when you're laid up with the flu
- see success as something you already have
- *Bhastrika,* or Bellows Breath, brings heat to the body and clears and purifies the body
- pick a newcomer to be on your team
- make your fears sit beside you instead of letting them hover over you
- practice reciprocity
- buy cold drinks for your entire row at a baseball game
- create a rotating six-year tax file
- refuse challenges to duel
- focus on those values and virtues that you know are important in the long run
- give things away
- decide that you are beautiful
- give a larger tip than normal
- explain patiently

- **don't agree when you don't**
- take a break from your desk and do a few free-weight exercises
- once a week, eat a liquefied diet
- toss to the winds your concern for this life
- mentally release tension through the soles of your feet
- give someone you love a back rub
- answers can often be worked out more skillfully when the mind is allowed to become quiet
- feel good about the things you decide to pursue
- volunteer as a counselor for a school or scout trip
- consider dropping "call waiting"
- practice with the kids for a family-bonding yoga session
- acknowledge your store of positive potential
- express kindness to foreign visitors
- encourage your spouse regularly
- phase out activities, habits, relationships that aren't as rewarding as others

529 instant karma

- build each day on a foundation of pleasant thoughts
- read only those books that are accepted without doubt as good
- pause for five minutes to pet a purring cat
- written teachings are a kind of food for your brain
- pray by breathing
- write a haiku
- spend time in activities that make you a better person
- the only thing you can ever really control is yourself
- adopt a forest
- use driving time as a chance to breathe and reflect
- help a person die well
- fight mold and mildew with tea tree oil
- place a geranium leaf on a painful ear to soothe it
- maintain an inventory of items stored in the basement or attic
- follow the example of those you admire most
- hail a taxi for an elderly person

- write legibly
- all three *doshas* (body types) should engage in yoga, walking, and swimming
- be creative in the face of problems
- give your guests what they never knew they wanted
- know that every right implies a responsibility
- practice genuine humility
- compliment yourself constantly
- sing while you play
- clarify your core values
- create breathing space
- practice tai chi movements like a cat taking a tentative step as it walks
- put vinegar on someone's sunburn
- thank someone for believing in you
- make sure your child is getting a good education
- let someone go ahead of you through revolving doors or onto the escalator

- create a vital documents "map" so you and everyone in the family can locate them
- preserve your car
- when you put your keys down, be conscious of putting them down; when you pick them up, be conscious of picking them up
- you have this precious human body in order to serve other living beings
- sing with exaltation
- speak and act as if everything you do is a real pleasure
- concentrate wholeheartedly
- realize that your "wasted day" was probably the break you needed
- make it a habit to do nice things for people who will never know it was you
- walk as if you are kissing the earth with your feet
- do a work marathon to catch up when you feel you are getting behind; you will feel better

- pursue a livelihood that directly contributes to the well-being of the world and enables you to more fully use your competitive capacities
- standing meditation is best learned from trees
- when you do something you are proud of, relish the experience
- join a pilgrimage
- respect wildlife
- love freely, purely
- require restaurant food to be fresh
- exfoliate your skin with a sea-salt paste accented with a blend of calming oils, such as lavender
- be kind and courteous to anyone who seems frazzled or short-tempered
- give a young child a large cardboard box to make a house or a car from
- let your kids pick out $100 worth of toys to give away to Toys for Tots

- learn how to open your heart to others
- make sure you have a clear view from the front entrance of your home
- tell someone you can't wait to experience whatever it is they are working on
- learn something new every day — or even more often!
- let someone else have the armrest on a plane or at the movies
- instead of regretting the past, create the future
- make sure you have the biggest smile in the world
- When in doubt, tell the truth (Mark Twain)
- you don't fail when you lose — you fail when you quit
- flow like a river toward the ocean, following the path of least resistance
- sacrifice for a good cause is karmically very favorable
- when you are with the person you love, be with the person you love without expecting anything
- risk getting hurt again

- list ten activities that you would like to do
- do what you can with what you have, wherever you are
- privately accumulate extraordinary knowledge and skill, but keep a plain appearance
- when you awake in the morning, breathe deeply and fill your insides with the emptiness around you
- every hour of this life should be lived in the best way you know how
- buy a roll of colored stickers and stick them on kids you know
- teach a child the alphabet, numbers, shapes, and colors
- on a weekend night, set the alarm for two A.M. to bake oatmeal cookies and read, write, or do whatever
- buy your son or daughter a desired piece of software
- make a point to pause and notice the world around you and inside you for one minute on the hour, every hour

- protect your enthusiasm from those who are negative
- be a wily observer of everything under the sun
- enjoy the gifts of others; each gives for his or her own reason
- give fresh flowers — since dried flowers may have negative energy from having died
- at the grocery store, thank the clerk and the bagger
- donate supplies or food to the local animal shelter/ rescue group
- keep your meditation experiences to yourself
- return a smile
- practice *jalandhara bandha:* while retaining the breath, press your chin firmly into the chest to help energy flow
- be clear and pure, utterly plain, and do not contrive artificialities but return to simplicity
- any positive change you make has the capacity to bear fruit

- accompany someone to an auction
- act on an intuitive feeling
- grow your own vegetables
- what are you putting into your body and why?
- take a friend to a yummy gourmet shop
- every moment conditions the arising of the next moment
- keep a birthday yearbook for a child, starting with the first birthday
- allow small disappointments to open unexpected doors
- simplicity brings more happiness than complexity
- live without envy
- be quiet while your partner watches his or her favorite show
- if at any time something doesn't feel right to you, why not honor your feelings?
- possess true grit and amazing grace

- have prescriptions filled for an older friend
- don't be "too grown up" for anything
- if something is worth doing, do it properly
- seize it all: what you seize is what you get
- like others, accept others, laugh with others
- welcome every morning with a smile
- acknowledge that everything you see is actually taking place, moment by moment, inside your own mind
- ask, "Will I even remember this situation in a few days, months, years?"
- lend a hand
- position a Buddha statue level with or higher than the occupants of the room
- give elbow room to others
- try tofu
- help save old trees
- keep a well-stocked sewing kit
- forgive quickly

- appreciate simple, satisfying tasks like straightening the clutter on your desk
- bounce back
- make a new employee feel welcome
- school never ends — the classroom is everywhere
- the fruit will bear a direct relationship to the seed
- think of your difficult times as spiritual training
- drink lots of water to boost your energy
- don't waste energy battling all the little waves — the ocean is full of them and they keep coming; just pay attention and correct the course when necessary
- clean out the refrigerator regularly
- welcome the unexpected
- find something to do
- offer comforting words after a nightmare
- be open and receive all the blessings meant for you
- take out the garbage when it's not your turn
- look into your children's eyes

- Be patient toward all that is unresolved in your heart and try to love the questions themselves (Rainer Maria Rilke)
- remember there are no stupid people in the world, just unhappy ones
- yoga is an invaluable tool in developing intuition
- do not force yourself to give up undesirable foods or deprive yourself by forced dieting
- fish kept in multiples of nine bring prosperity
- examine your felt need to accumulate and hold on to things
- lose all desire for things beyond your reach
- seek happiness in solitude
- sit up straight; practice good posture
- raise children who respect the earth
- honor those in authority
- awaken the mind without fixing it anywhere
- go back to school for an advanced degree

instant karma 540

- let no items enter your kingdom that are frivolous or will needlessly complicate your life
- it takes twenty-one days of practicing a new behavior before it becomes a habit
- work toward a smoke-free world
- pick up the check
- serve breakfast in bed and don't worry about the mess
- find the idea for which you can live and die
- seek a gentler life
- be honest, fair, and kind as you move along
- write a personal mission statement to inspire yourself, not to impress anyone else
- treasure life as a gift
- heal a breach
- consider journal-keeping, to help you know yourself better
- switch to natural ingredients, certified organic products, foods that are not genetically modified

- help someone practice a skill
- give a soft answer even when you feel strongly
- have the courage to let go and trust in your life's natural flow
- express something deep within yourself by writing
- maintain a depth of commitment that can be sustained over the long haul
- take care of plants
- look for something beautiful in one person each day
- save someone a place in line
- agree to disagree
- only the truth will set you free
- make a list of all the things you'd like to do or become in this life, then do whatever is necessary to realize them
- hold a koan in your mind while meditating
- when you make the connection between all things, you have a way out of isolation

- laugh off a ridiculous situation
- visit home often
- send flowers anonymously to someone who could use cheering up
- speak gently and sincerely
- get some insight
- keep your promises
- be happily alone in a crowd
- spend two weeks climbing in the Sierras with Outward Bound
- take time to think
- savor big joys and small pleasures
- stand up for your own rights
- help clean a polluted beach
- develop a fitness program for yourself
- be a useful person
- use the power of your imagination every day
- hang out with your kids

- refrain from packing your life too full of activities and projects
- If you can manage to be nice to people, this is enough (Dalai Lama)
- ask other people about themselves
- walk on alone even if you have no support on the spiritual path
- encourage children to celebrate their own uniqueness
- make your own perfume
- whenever anyone lightens your load, be sure to thank that person
- give employees stipends for saving the company money
- thank doormen
- visualize a mountain to deepen concentration and mindfulness in sitting practice
- think about ways you can deepen your commitment to those values you hold most dear
- keep all rooms free from clutter, even the basement

- promote peace, education, and reconciliation within families, communities, nations, and in the world
- share your lunch
- celebrate today
- give your time and talents to causes you believe in
- the only mistake is not to learn from a mistake
- learn a foreign language by tape in the car
- be friends with your sister or brother
- use a secret "I love you" signal with family members
- make a dream come true
- give water to a thirsty person
- spoil the birthday boy or girl
- follow your vision to the end despite all the obstacles in your way
- act as if it is your duty to be happy
- believe in the dignity of labor
- practice *nadi shodhana,* or alternate nostril breathing, to balance your emotional and physical natures

- your life is the path
- take a child to work
- bury a treasure for a child and make a map to find it
- ask if someone has lost weight
- know when enough is enough
- have a lit-from-within glow
- repetition and absorption of sound leads to sacredness
- set up a first aquarium for a child
- visualize what you want to manifest in your life
- empty the trash nightly without being asked
- say "Breathing in, I calm my anger. Breathing out, I take care of my anger."
- when you buy a new piece of clothing, get rid of one old piece
- whichever form of feng shui you choose, be consistent and practical
- keep your dealings with others as straightforward as possible

- obey the law even when a cop is not around
- Not to be attached to something is to be aware of its absolute value (Shunryu Suzuki Roshi)
- seek knowledge to plan, enterprise to execute, honesty to govern all
- never retaliate
- be at peace regardless of the other person's disposition
- learn to massage your own neck, shoulders, and feet
- stop craving material things
- practice Downward Dog to explore proper alignment and help bring blood back to the heart
- give yourself the chance to start over
- it is better to give than to receive
- once committed, give it all you've got
- work at allowing more things to unfold in your life without forcing them to happen or rejecting things that should not be happening
- remember that the best things in life are free

- things are never as bad as you imagine them to be
- take a small gift when invited to a friend's house
- nothing is troublesome that we do willingly
- understand your own emotions and how they affect your behavior
- there are three elements — thought, speech, actions — with which karma is made
- have great non-expectations
- play nice background music
- don't be critical of your loved ones' friends
- give someone peace and quiet
- avoid overload, which leaves you feeling dull
- write moral fables
- kiss your spouse under the mistletoe
- take the kids on a foliage-viewing trip
- read Alan Lakein's *How to Get Control of Your Time and Your Life*
- when there is selfishness, offer generosity

- if you are religious, affirm your faith each day
- offer perfectly reasonable explanations
- donate an unused swing set to a day-care center
- remember that decency and inner beauty are more valuable than appearance
- be a leader when you see a path others have missed
- videotape a big event for someone
- use the inner to make the external enjoyable, but do not use externals to make the inner enjoyable
- try to keep the right posture in all your activities
- practice preventive medicine
- use self-love as your only weight-loss aid
- take your child on a secret surprise destination car ride
- call a wise sibling for advice
- buy only nonviolent video games
- keep your eye on the rearview mirror
- sell unused clothing on consignment
- memorize only clean jokes

- try not to force an idea on others, but rather think about it with them and let them change their own minds
- become aware of how you feel when you eat
- resist the impulse to interfere unnecessarily with outcomes
- even in the most difficult circumstances, do not complain, panic, or lose hope
- re-create your first date
- you get back from the world exactly what you put into the world
- Work is much more fun than fun (Noël Coward)
- take a kid to a paint-your-own-ceramics studio
- mend a quarrel
- most things you feel bad about weren't so bad to begin with
- see if you can still do fifty sit-ups
- manage your time well

- be ruthless about clearing away material you no longer need
- make chocolate pudding for a kid with a cold
- dispose of batteries properly
- take an art course every year
- build a dream and the dream builds you
- believe in the possibility of happiness
- train your mind to desire what the situation demands
- close your eyes when you kiss
- sink into yourself and find refuge there
- The quieter you become, the more you can hear (Ram Dass)
- visualize success, visualize health
- encourage a youth to do his or her best
- file as much as you can electronically
- Seize today, and put a little trust as you can in the morrow (Horace)
- go on a picnic

 551 instant karma

- leave every person you come into contact with feeling better
- help a city repossess a vacant building to use for the underprivileged or the elderly
- learn to unwind
- learn the power of restraint
- join a social organization that does good for a group or the community
- do a laughing meditation
- decide for yourself
- have the grace to refrain from an unkind word
- lower your voice
- do a good job at whatever challenges you face
- spend less time on the phone
- be quiescent
- envision your protective bubble staying with you whatever you do
- keep a long-range perspective

- live with the knowledge that you've done your best
- start to think in a positive way and you will immediately experience an upturn in fortune
- retreat when necessary
- resolve to no longer react negatively to whatever happens around you
- take a walk in the rain and really experience it
- fight the defamation of homosexuals
- communicate unconditional love
- play fair
- be open to "what is" instead of "what if"
- sit in a chair, hands on thighs, breathing through your nose and concentrate on your third eye — visualizing a triangle between it and your hands
- choose beverages and foods to moderate your intake of sugars
- celebrate the holidays of all the religions
- if you have to eat at McDonald's, order a Happy Meal

- refurbish a child's old sled
- be open to sights, smells, and sounds
  in your immediate environment
- when life gives you roadblocks, take healthy detours
- improve elder care through nursing homes,
  hospitals, and Alzheimer's organizations
- walk to allow yourself to tap into insights
  you may not have realized you have
- do away with overreacting
- bless sneezers
- look at the world as a mirage,
  as a bubble floating in front of you
- abstain from using food as a courage crutch
- live on half of what you earn and save the other half
- wear nice pajamas, just as you wear nice clothes
- spend a Saturday afternoon at a bowling alley
- practice tai chi regularly to help you become more
  aware of your body

instant karma 554

- choose to love someone right now
- treat yourself to uplifting plays, films, performances
- do something positive for the inner city
- lend a sympathetic ear
- whenever you make a mistake or get knocked down by life, don't look back at it too long
- travel lighter
- want the best for people
- develop an ability to make life better or more special
- how can you make your situation more fun?
- use the sound of the mantra *om mani padme hum* to subdue negative energy
- break large tasks into smaller tasks
- make the bed
- simply be happy
- cat meals under the trees
- remember that true labor is half initiative and half knowing how to let things proceed on their own

 instant karma

- give your children both roots and wings
- love the rain
- stop trying to change people
- share a roll of Life Savers
- create imaginary allies
- never punish yourself
- take lots of deep breaths
- allow someone who needs cheering up to cry
- ask for what you want
- be easily contented
- take a curious, receptive nonvegetarian friend out to a vegetarian restaurant
- practice visualization after meditation, yoga, or exercise
- learn life's lessons with a light heart
- give little love gifts
- support your local sports teams
- support equal rights

- mist your feet with a blend of tea tree and eucalyptus oils
- embrace aloneness and solitude, realizing you are one with the universe
- applaud our veterans
- be friendly but respect others' space
- use money you win to help others
- sample Gonsen koans, which help clarify the difficult words of Zen masters and open a hidden world of beauty and wisdom
- allow your mate to "lose it" every once in a while
- engage in energy-renewing activities
- do your duty, even when critical eyes watch
- everyone can learn from your kindness, and everyone deserves your kindness
- ask, "What am I waiting for to make me happy? Why am I not happy right now?"
- after a misunderstanding, be the first to say "I'm sorry"

- look at the problems in the world: is your problem really as big as you think?
- wean yourself off salt by using herbs and spices
- take a wellness day — a paid personal day or unpaid day off — to do whatever you want
- cultivate the art of never complaining
- pick more daisies
- let your goals evolve with your life circumstances
- throw away your pitiful apathy and act boldly in a crisis
- support the local newspaper, no matter its quality
- keep a fire burning as a welcome
- invent new ways to love
- the people we love need space in order to be happy
- don't be preoccupied with appearance
- clean a shoreline
- have picnics rather than go to a restaurant
- create a compassionate, humorous label for an insistent thought, such as "The-I-Blew-It-Again Story"

- believe you can have a contented mind
- defer to those who are more enlightened than you are
- load up on greens and veggies
- breathe in, smile, breathe out, let go
- attempt easy tasks as if they were difficult and difficult tasks as if they were easy
- keep your private thoughts private
- if you're in a hole, quit digging deeper
- follow the six guiding principles of Pilates: concentration, control, centering, flow, precision, and breathing
- can you let this go?
- burn a red candle for protection
- develop a strong wish to refrain from harming others, either physically or verbally, no matter what
- have a comfort drawer of little things that make you feel pampered and cared for
- offer someone the cherry from your drink

- read, sing, listen to your children
- head out for a "random drive"
- vow that once you sit down to meditation, all disturbances will stop
- open up all your senses
- ring a bell in the corners of a room to clear stagnant or stale energy
- rethink your plan of action when things get too complicated
- instead of running errands, stroll them
- believe in ultimate justice — in karma
- recognize when things are ripe, and know how to enjoy them
- help with a science project
- pause before your emotions take over your actions
- do a craft with kids, especially one for an upcoming holiday
- we are solely responsible for our own cure

- take the time to wait; dawdle in the present tense
- help a turtle cross the street
- only when you empty out your teacup can you make room for the really good tea
- always leave loved ones with loving words
- try the foot push exercise for abdominals
- carry only the load of the moment, no more than that
- deepen your love of wisdom
- debate half in jest
- allow your mind the freedom to not know for a period of time
- let go of winning and losing and find joy
- put a halt to excessive toy buying
- tell yourself, "Because I am calm and relaxed, I can handle any problem."
- make sure you tip the people who deliver the newspaper at daybreak each morning of the year
- work to level the playing field

- when you feel true gratitude, *metta* (loving-kindness) will flow from you naturally
- seek to understand your mistakes so that you may not repeat them
- learn from situations that make you feel anxious or impatient
- give yourself time with friends, doing what you want to do
- learn to use what happens to you instead of trying to control what happens to you
- refraining from wrong speech means not only telling the truth but avoiding useless and frivolous talk
- polish your social skills
- inquiry brings a dash of zest to life
- rise to the occasion and fight bravely for what is right
- always do what you are afraid to do
- resolve for five minutes to let your mind appear as a blank screen and watch for thoughts

- seek and find quiet
- take care of the thoughts, and the actions will take care of themselves
- exist for the good of man
- consciously direct your breathing to each of the seven chakras, spending two minutes at each energy center
- release any beliefs that have outlived their usefulness
- communicate in a way that fosters connection rather than divisiveness
- make flash cards to help a child study
- create a mental sanctuary
- when someone expresses a need, do something about it
- wash a baby in Ivory soap
- don't confuse your life and your work; the second is only part of the first
- give your time to help the local charity thrift store
- toast marshmallows with the kids

- proclaim the good qualities and achievements
  of others
- your invisible work on your own improvement
  is the most important work in the world
- drink at least three glasses of water before lunchtime
- on your way to and from work, listen to all
  the sounds around you without judgment
- be free to change and express yourself
- be careful not to criticize or fight the mind
- don't eat to dullness
- ask, "How do I live my life in the best way?"
- realize that you don't have power over what happens,
  but you do control your attitude
- visit an art gallery and buy a colorful postcard
  or poster reproduction
- ride a carousel
- work toward improving recreational opportunities
  in your area

instant karma 564

- organize safe trick-or-treating
- minimize talk about work matters
- display patience in front of children
- take a stand
- love your mother-in-law and father-in-law
- expect a miracle
- there is always another option
- throw a birthday party for a friend
- tread softly to go far
- raise money to help care for others in need
- when you start to pay attention, your relationship to things deepens
- buy foods that are made from natural products
- reach out to help without waiting for someone to ask
- contribute money and goods to feed the hungry
- your conduct is crucial
- make a long-term pledge to practice letting go of grudges

- sing "and many more" at the end of "Happy Birthday"
- enrich your environment through sound:
  play music a lot
- donate good books to a nursing home
- try not to eat for at least six hours before bedtime
- thank your in-laws for raising your spouse as they did
- be a crusader for love
- revise some favorite meat-based recipes to make them
  vegetarian
- change your clothes to rid yourself of the day's *chi*
- if you catch a fish, throw it back in
- stretch and fire up your muscles before getting out
  of bed
- you need more wisdom, not knowledge, and wisdom
  comes from attention
- focus on living a quality life
- encourage would-be artists
- always put something in the collection plate or can

- love many things with a passion
- carve out personal time for yourself
- accomplish great tasks by a series of small acts
- choose a charity and support it in any way you can
- allow snuggle time in your bed when you wake up on the weekend
- promote non-electronic children's playtime
- you may stumble, but you must always get up again
- take pleasure in giving to others
- wake up your mind by doing something new
- watch a bird build its nest
- read books on your child's reading list
- find ways to integrate your spiritual philosophy into your relationships
- offer to spend an evening with an elderly person so the caregiver can have a night off
- keep a good book by your bedside
- put on a puppet show for a sick child

- expect to remember what you read
- make a new friend of an old person
- sing "Amazing Grace" to lift your spirits
- instead of eliminating desires, seek to transform them
- eat together often as a family
- take a child to a hobby shop
- don't put on airs or try to impress anyone
- beware of routines
- take a calcium supplement
- keep spending records
- volunteer to play games with children in a hospital
- be a stabilizing force for someone else
- believe in the sacredness of a promise
- share the abundance of your garden
- slow down and reevaluate what's important
- remain in a state of perpetual meditation
- move your workout area to the center
  of the room for good feng shui

instant karma 568

- bring your pet to a nursing home for a visit
- grow courage
- we are a result of our past lives, but we are also a result of what we did yesterday
- be prompt with get-well cards and expressions of sympathy
- help a child to enjoy a holiday for the right reasons
- sweep someone's driveway when the person is not there
- discipline with love
- focus on your main duty
- do it right the first time
- the wisest among us have the least to say
- organize a litter pickup or litter patrol
- cook dinner with a dear friend
- spend your retirement as a volunteer for good causes
- ask for nothing and give everything
- tie up loose ends before concluding your workday

- help a child with hiccups
- confront conflict without shame
- teach ethics
- make time alone together after the children are asleep
- intellectually try and test everything that can possibly be put to the test
- write your troubles in sand and watch the water make them disappear
- stop believing your inner critic
- study comparative religion
- for dinner, eat light and early
- donate used bikes
- put a blanket over someone who is napping
- allot part of your lunch period to movement — walk, yoga, light aerobics
- request a White House birthday greeting for someone turning eighty
- listen to grandparents' stories

instant karma 570

- "adopt" a highway
- select an appropriate posture for meditation and do it correctly
- show a child how much fun life can be
- make someone else feel valuable
- in walking, just walk; in sitting, just sit
- buy tickets to see your favorite comedian/comedienne
- you never lose what you share and give away
- have an impact on people
- create a place where you can work on a hobby to your heart's content
- do Taoist breathing, directing your inhalation into the area four finger widths below the navel and extending your exhalation
- see and let go
- your behavior while no one is watching reveals your true character
- make "natural" Christmas tree ornaments

- be an adventure
- try to acquire as few new problems as possible
- work to become, not to acquire
- be unfinicky
- sip tea throughout the day to hydrate your body
- make to-do maps (making logical connections and associations) instead of lists
- buck a trend
- give a back scratch or neck rub
- join a glee club
- meet the need of the moment, even when it is not your need
- allow ideas to ripen
- be a good friend
- try to understand someone
- truly learn when you study
- light your altar on special occasions
- experience the void or non-self of inner stillness

- remember that almost anything can be done if you proceed slowly enough
- help your children create a good self-image
- let go — because there is nothing worth holding on to
- preserve country roads instead of paving them
- set up a romantic scavenger hunt, steering your lover to a restaurant or back home for a private celebration
- say "good morning" in the morning
- let your child select one night's dinner menu, especially the dessert
- have a clear plan every day as to what you want to accomplish
- your past and future simultaneously exist in your present — so be present!
- respect others' sleeping hours
- carry someone's backpack
- be an organ donor
- smile all the time

- respect the flag
- do the things that make you feel good about yourself
- try to live in balance
- compassion is an awareness and determination that demands action
- remove the internal emotional hooks that attach you to painful situations
- appreciate having the house all to yourself
- take a grandparent to the movies
- make something worthwhile out of the common clay of your life
- volunteer at the Special Olympics
- display an appropriate sense of humor
- answer questions sincerely
- share the credit
- sit with your legs crossed, arms out like wings, and flap your wrists/hands rapidly for three minutes (for the sixth chakra)

- do your duty
- show trust
- help a youngster learn new skills or improve in a weak area
- learn to touch the earth more gently
- can you carry the mountain image with you in daily life?
- take a mini-vacation in a rocking chair
- reach out to those you've learned from and say thank you
- give a kid a vacation of a lifetime
- become more in touch with your hands in sitting meditation
- look through the thought, not at it
- trust your kids to do the right thing
- have joie de vivre
- take time each afternoon for a cup of tea and reflection

- let the fresh air in and the stale air out
- grow sunflowers
- win a prize for a child at a fair
- in everything you encounter in your life, ask yourself, "What kinds of life food am I eating?"
- find your weaknesses and fix them
- have faith — in yourself, your family, your friends, the world
- attempt to improve educational systems
- notice what opportunities to serve come your way
- when you feel rooted in something, you feel at home and empowered
- set physical goals for yourself
- establish an attitude of contentment during meditation
- stop working overtime
- put the needs of others first
- practice letting go of the urge to eat when you're not hungry

- secretly plant tulip bulbs all over the neighborhood
- attend high school plays and musical productions
- tell someone you love him or her while you still have the chance
- rent a romantic film classic and light a fire
- stop at a new place for coffee or flowers
- teach your child the art of sharing
- look for friendly faces
- end every yoga session with a few minutes of complete, total relaxation
- stretch your arms and legs — a lot
- if you're told a secret, keep it
- admire wildflowers alongside a highway
- start or add to someone's library of cookbooks
- notice individual raindrops
- keep your vows
- give others the benefit of the doubt
- cheerfully greet all employees with a smile each day

- face discomfort, greet it, and go with it until it matures into accomplishment, pride, satisfaction
- kiss your spouse before leaving the house
- to receive love, be loving
- listen to a child practice and rehearse
- make plans, not resolutions
- ask advice from a youngster
- relax and enjoy the ride
- listen to good music from famous musicians
- split the chores with others
- hold more hands
- ask yourself, "Will this matter a year from now?"
- teach your children a second language
- care about the smallest details in a piece of marble or wood
- do the thing you have to do, when it ought to be done, whether you like it or not
- work to preserve open space

- get rid of things or you'll spend your whole life tidying up
- self-awareness leads to self-control
- the greatest cure is to give up, to relinquish, to surrender
- whatever you can do or dream you can, begin it
- learn from the skilled
- remember that kids take note of everything adults do and say
- develop a penchant for hard work
- learn to drink and stay sober, by appreciating what you drink
- pick your own apples or berries
- accept strong emotions in others and do not take responsibility for them
- do exercise that you love
- don't criticize, condemn, or complain
- show respect for elders

- when tempted to criticize your parent, spouse, or children, bite your tongue
- ginger aids digestion and stimulates circulation
- practice visualization when your body is relaxed and your mind is free
- tai chi stresses inward focus and moving slowly through forms that require balance and control
- take advantage of quiet time on a bus
- watch uplifting movies
- simply soak up the day
- increase proportions of vegetable in recipes
- take a young child fishing at the lake
- positive results stem from a combination of physical activity and mental calmness, as in qigong
- you do not require perfect quiet to meditate; it isn't noise that bothers you, it is your judgment about the noise
- get your responsibilities behind you

- eat no more than one or two servings a day of lean meat (fish, chicken, turkey, pork, beef)
- make your world your monastery — wherever you are, whatever you encounter is meant to provide you with exactly what you need right now
- you are what you believe
- go snorkeling to get a different perspective on the world
- give kids tried-and-true gifts that tend to have more lasting value than the latest fad
- make yourself necessary to someone
- Happiness never decreases by being shared (Buddha)
- favor products that are durable, easy to repair, energy-efficient, and functional
- the food you eat affects your vital energy, mental capabilities, and emotional health as well as your physical well-being
- seek the wisdom the world holds

- cut grass, shovel snow, chop wood, rake leaves —
  these are all grounding activities
- laugh often and love much
- find the time to keep a promise
- read, meditate, study, paint, garden, sculpt, swim,
  write, bake, play tennis, go to a museum
- become flexible, physically and mentally
- give your compliments to the chef
- make a commitment to daily self-cultivation
- anything worthwhile requires a certain amount
  of sacrifice
- wake up to classical music
- take a meditation class
- give yourself free time in which to let your mind
  wander
- involve yourself with good people
- change the name of the main character in
  a read-aloud book to your child's name

- encourage the miraculous by believing in the impossible
- eat all your meals away from the television, computer, and telephone
- buy prepared sage sticks in a health food store and walk through your house with the stick lit; this is called "smudging," and it purifies the energy in your aura
- tell kids that you trust them
- call your two favorite people to tell them how wonderful they are
- For I have learned, in whatsoever state I am therewith to be content (Philippians 4:11)
- do your work, then step back; it's the only path to serenity
- be ready for the unforeseen
- spread all the good news that you can
- sit on the seashore and listen to the surf
- make a list of 100 questions that are important to you

- cultivate a boundless heart toward all beings
- come to a complete stop
- leave the world a bit better
- cut toxic people out of your life
- enjoy your unique combination of mind and body
- if you want people to do more, praise and appreciate what they are already doing
- keep an eye on kids in a swimming pool
- an act of meditation is actually an act of faith — faith in your own potential
- play with your pet
- do the yoga Cat/Cow Pose on all fours — and breathe
- Every moment is a golden one for him who has the vision to recognize it as such (Henry Miller)
- make spirits bright
- one song can spark a moment
- learn the vocabulary of your passionate interest
- face the truth

- put a note in someone's pocket with a list of things to be happy about
- snuggle in a bathrobe while reading a good book
- omit needless words
- commit to advancing a better world
- give your mind the freedom it needs to take you beyond suffering
- make yourself interesting
- offer good wishes to each being you meet
- leave a love note for family members for each day you'll be away on a trip
- send a sympathy card to a child who has lost a pet
- a person's name is to that person the sweetest sound
- read a page from an inspirational book each morning
- just one great idea can revolutionize your life
- take things in stride
- hang mistletoe to assure many kisses in your house
- donate a basketball to a local youth recreation center

585 instant karma

- make a quilt for your kid or grandkid
- be the same privately as you are publicly
- every so often, let your spirit of adventure take over
- take off your blinders
- acknowledge another's point of view
- keep a well-stocked school/office supply kit
- become one with each yoga pose
- schedule fun
- create an island of being in the sea of constant doing
- the decision to change has a beauty in itself
- refrain from praising your own qualities and achievements
- sell books you no longer use
- grow professionally and personally
- send encouraging notes
- have a positive effect on people
- choose the longest line at the grocery store or bank — breathe slowly and focus on your impatience

instant karma 586

- support organic farming
- let your negative thoughts go, wish your enemies well (even in the privacy of your own mind)
- A great man shows his greatness by the way he treats little men (Thomas Carlyle)
- try yoga's 61-Point Relaxation Exercise, a relaxation of the body in numerical order of points
- learn from every person that you meet
- remember that you are only as flexible as your spine
- you are your karma
- identify less with the changing physical shell and more with your spirit
- put a moratorium on shopping — limiting your purchases to groceries and bare essentials — for thirty days
- call to check on someone when he is sick
- support a recovering alcoholic
- each day presents a new opportunity for awakening

- every time a thought arises, throw it away
- keep your eyes and ears open to get the messages you need
- smooth, rounded, worry stones passed finger-to-finger focus the mind and calm anxiety
- see for yourself
- when you are sad, do the one thing that really makes you happy
- *chi* travels best along curving paths, not around angles and sharp corners
- kiss children good night, even if they are already asleep
- challenge the rules
- strive valiantly
- watch your intentions before performing routine activities
- to eat in the Zen way, every bite and crumb should be fully and completely tasted
- never take any loving relationship for granted

- forgiveness is at the heart of all happiness
- just because your emotions rise up, doesn't mean you have to follow
- be a reading role model
- help at a senior center once a week
- relax into life
- notice the slightest of noises, movements, shifts of light
- clean your pet's teeth
- know that not everything needs to be said
- burn a green candle to heal energies and bring luck and prosperity
- get to know people
- take Christmas cookies to friends
- partake only in constructive doubt
- set goals that are ambitious but achievable
- give your partner a single long-stemmed rose
- request a birthday greeting on someone's favorite radio station

- set an alcohol-free "happy hour" for yourself each day
- a releasing breath — breathing in through your nose and forcefully breathing out through your mouth — gets your anger and frustrations out
- renew your wedding vows
- pardon errors
- discipline with a gentle hand
- if you are in a dream world, zap yourself back to reality
- go for it — lock, stock, and barrel
- air out your house and add some fragrant flowers
- put socks on a sleeping child so the feet will be warm when the child wakes up
- do hands-on hobbies like woodwork, painting, or cooking
- give yourself a day off
- glimpse the infinite emptiness surrounding you
- choose a job you love
- delegate dinner duty

- mute your mind
- take a daily vitamin supplement
- join in celebrations that are meaningful to those close to you
- get through rush-hour traffic with a smile
- learn to endure the small things
- understand the origins of your religion
- allow someone the luxury of sleeping late
- offer your newspaper or magazine to someone as you leave a waiting area
- see poetry in everything
- the only reason we are on earth is to learn, and karma provides the lessons
- What is not easy to do should be done with great persistence (Confucius)
- Life is ten percent what happens to me and ninety percent how I react to it (Lou Holtz)
- what makes you feel good can also make you look good

 instant karma

- every great thing is done in a quiet, humble, simple way
- catch the romance of the moment
- respect each child's style
- stay happily married for a lifetime
- wait your turn
- thank your spouse regularly
- redefining a goal does not mean that you have failed, only that you have learned from your experience
- spend time with people who think you're splendid and who tell you so
- keep the child within you alive
- fire your imagination with small details
- celebrate all of your birthdays no matter how old you get
- use rainy days for special projects that you have been putting off
- let your own inherent gentleness free you

- decide which battles are worth fighting and which are better left alone
- look into bodywork techniques: Trager Approach, Aston-Patterning, and Hellerwork
- hire people who like people
- give a Chinese unicorn as a present to bestow good wishes upon someone
- have some great fallback meals in the freezer, like veggie French bread pizza
- love the tools with which you work
- to revive energy and spirit in the afternoon, try self-massage, yoga, tai chi, and/or breathing exercises
- if you go on an all-out binge, immediately return to three meals a day
- do whatever is needed for the well-being of the biosphere
- encourage a child to learn something
- the less said about life's suffering, the better

- the way you eat, drink and walk in daily life impact the world
- find any excuse to get outdoors
- wear clothes that you love
- the best beauty product is to have a real life
- use your energy positively
- help save a "lost soul"
- smother your mate with kisses
- keep your house full of flowers
- cherish your friends
- sing with gusto
- start where you are

ABOUT THE AUTHOR

Barbara Ann Kipfer is the author of more than twenty-five books. She holds master's degrees in Buddhist studies and linguistics, and doctorates in linguistics and archaeology. Besides several Workman books, including the bestselling *14,000 Things to be Happy About,* she has written many reference books. She creates good karma as a lexicographer and archaeologist living in Connecticut with her family.